MW01293170

Things Pondered From a Mother's Heart

Lauren Mitchell

Things Pondered From A Mother's Heart
Copyright © 2012
Lauren Mitchell

Published by Flint River Collective
Brooks, Georgia

All rights reserved. No part of this publication may be reproduced, stored in a retrieval system, or transmitted in any form by any means, electronic, mechanical, photocopy, recording, or otherwise, without the prior permission of the publication, except as provided by USA copyright law.

Cover design: Dylan Higgins
Second Printing 2015
Printed in the United States of America

ISBN-13: 978-1477511596
ISBN-10: 1477511598

Scripture quotations are from The Holy Bible, English Standard Version® (ESV®), copyright © 2001 by Crossway, a publishing ministry of Good News Publishers. Used by permission. All rights reserved.

DEDICATION

This book is dedicated to my children, Kate and Brian. God has used them in the most instrumental ways in my life. They never cease to be a joy and blessing.

CONTENTS

ACKNOWLEDGMENTS

Pete, I want to thank you for being my rock. God gave you to me because he knew how much I needed you. Kaycee, I want to thank you for believing in me. Lorey, thanks for being my editor but first my friend and encourager. This book served to give us roots. I also want to thank my Bible study girls for their prayers and endless support. I love you girls.

FORWARD

Even in the, sometimes, mundane lives of mothers, God provides countless revelations of Truth.

The following are short stories from the heart of a mother who has learned to take the time she is given with her children and use it to listen to the heart of God. My children have been more instrumental in showing me the face of God and his love for me than I could have imagined. Jesus also uses them to teach me things about myself I needed, but hadn't wanted to see. Children are a blessing from the Lord because of the glimpses they give us of God's heart for us. He uses mine to teach me lessons everyday. These are all simple thoughts from a mother's heart. "For prophecy never had it's origin in the will of man, but men spoke from God as they were carried along by the Holy Spirit." Through this journey, I have been carried along by the Holy Spirit. I want to open your eyes to God all around you. I just started with children. They are a wealth of knowledge, the kind you can't get in any book.

"But Mary treasured up all these things, pondering them in her heart."
Luke 2:19

DAY 1
As Little Children

"He said to them; Let the little children come to me,
and do not hinder them,
for the kingdom of God belongs to such as these.
I tell you the truth; anyone who will not receive the kingdom
of God like a little child will never enter it.
And he took the children in his arms,
put his hands on them and blessed them."
Mark 10:14-16

The reflections compiled in this book are dear to my heart because they are lessons God implanted in my life. They are like hidden treasures in my daily life to remind me of His presence and plan. He is there. He takes the mundane and ordinary of every day life and makes it extraordinary. That is why I want to share them with you. God is after your heart, and He plants lessons in your life to lead you. They are there just for you. They are hidden all around us. All of nature cries out that there is a Creator. He created children as a blessing, not just for our enjoyment but also our instruction. They teach us things if we watch. We assume that they learn from us, when in reality we have much to learn from them. Heaven is hidden all around us. "I thank you, Father, Lord of heaven and earth, that you have hidden these things from the wise and understanding and revealed them to little children" (Matthew 11:25).

I have learned more about God from my children than I would ever have imagined. Some days I really want to put them in the freezer and keep them right here at this age. I want to preserve what makes them so precious and lovable. It's not just their midget size and the way they run. It's not just chubby fingers with dimples. It's not just their ability to laugh until they can't breathe at being tickled or just getting tickled over something and giggling forever. They are delighted by the simplest things. They are not complex. They have a clear understanding of loyalty and truth. They know what it means to love. Children are yet untainted by the world. I think God looks at us just this way. He knows we must grow up, yet He doesn't want us to lose the innate qualities of children. We must mature in Christ just like in life; yet keep that clarity and innocence. He cherishes in us that same laughter that I cherish in my children, and He loves when we trust Him enough to run with abandon in the direction He has called us. This is how we become like little children, so that we may receive the kingdom. "The kingdom of heaven belongs to such as these."

If you have lost the ability to gut laugh, jump on the bed, dance like you mean it, or run like crazy for sheer joy; only He can restore it. He will, if you ask. "I run in the path of your commands, for you have set my heart free" (Psalm 119:32). Jesus can set your heart free.

Children followed Jesus because they knew He was real. He wasn't like other adults. Children have an uncanny sense of discernment for sincerity. Simply put, they can spot a fake a mile away. In Matthew chapter 21 Jesus gives us an example. The children knew who He was. They were proclaiming, "Hosanna to the son of David" (v. 15). The chief priests and teachers of the law came to Jesus and said, "Do you hear what these children are saying?"(v. 16). Jesus responded, "Yes, have you never read, 'From the lips of children and infants you have ordained praise?'" The signs were given and the chief priests and the teachers of the law should have been the first to see them, but they weren't. "We speak of God's secret wisdom, a wisdom that has been hidden and that God destined for our glory before time began. None of the rulers of this age understood it, for if they had, they would not have crucified the Lord of glory" (1 Corinthians 2:7&8). I want to grasp what those children had because I don't want to miss God's wisdom. These stories are simply the lessons God has hidden for me in my children. They have taught me about God and myself through their unfettered lives. They show me God's heart and what is in my own heart. They show me sometimes how I was meant to be, and other times they are a picture of why I am so desperate for Jesus. I have much more to learn from them, and I don't want to miss any of it.

"How great is the love the Father has lavished on us, that we should be called the children of God! And that is what we are! The reason the world does not know us is that it did not know him."
1 John3:1

> "My son, if you accept my words
> and store up my commands within you,
> turning your ear to wisdom
> and applying your heart to understanding,
> and if you call out for insight
> and cry aloud for understanding
> and if you look for it as silver
> and search for it as for *hidden treasure*,
> then you will understand the fear of the Lord
> and find the knowledge of God."
> (emphasis added) Proverbs 2:1-5

God open our hearts and unstop our ears so that we can clearly discern what comes from you, in whatever form it may come. Make us keenly aware of your presence in the mundane of our lives. In that awareness of you, we won't miss the truth you plant in our path everyday. Help us receive that truth like little children.

DAY 2
<u>Crying Under Cribs</u>

My daughter can't see me, so she cries frantic, pathetic cries, while shaking the bars of her crib. She is sure I have abandoned her behind her bars. In her eight months of life, I have never abandoned her before, but she is positive I have now. She can't see, hear, or smell me. In her limited vision, I am gone. She proceeds to scream at the top of her lungs. It is a cry of complete exhaustion; and if she would just give in and shut her eyes, she would collapse in a peaceful rest, but she won't let go. If you entered the room right now, you would laugh at the picture we make. The scene would find me lying on the floor, under Kate's crib. When she cries, I cry. I tell myself, "It is for her own good. She needs rest." More tears follow, more mine than hers. Kate is my first child, and when she cries, I have a painful gut reaction. I assure you it is a physical reaction. Every mother knows the feeling. Doing something for your child's good is never easy. I remember my parents saying, "This hurts me more than you." I just thought it was an expression! I was so wrong!

Just like Kate, I am sometimes sure God must have abandoned me. Though He has never done it before, in my limited vision, I can't see, hear, or smell him. He is no less there because I cannot perceive Him. Though I may feel alone, God is right there. Though I don't understand what is happening, He does. Though I don't want it any more than Kate wants her nap, He knows I need this season. As much as I love Kate, God loves me more. Hear that: God loves us more than we love our own children. Do you believe that? Sometimes knowing that something is true doesn't make us act like it is. God feels my pain when I cry. It hurts Him just as much as it hurts me when Kate cries. It is almost a physical pain reaction when I hear her. God loves us like that. He knows that I must go through life's pain to become sanctified through and through (1 Thessalonians 5:23). He is faithful; He will do it (v. 24). He will do what is best for us, even when He feels the pain. Just like making Kate sleep when she doesn't want to leads to her health and well being, so God's love for us must lead to the same thing. Otherwise, He would be leaving us to run our own agenda, and it would be the same end result as a child who runs their own agenda.

That day, under the crib, I was struck with a thought. Nobody told me that being a parent would be this hard. If someone had really explained it to me, I might have been more prepared. God knew what it would involve when He chose me to be His child, and He knew what it would cost; He chose to be my parent anyway. He knew exactly what it would cost to redeem me, and He still chose me. He knew I needed a shepherd, and He is willing to be it. He knew before he chose to be my Father that I would cause him pain. He chose it anyway; just like I choose to love my children despite the pain. I just need to quit screaming at the top of my lungs and trust that He is there. When I am having a fit like Kate, it puts me in two places. One: I can't hear a word God says because I can only hear myself. Two: I can't feel any comfort. God cannot hold me if I refuse to stop flailing my arms. He is there waiting to give me rest, but I can't accept it as long as I scream and demand my own way. God instructs us to, "Be still and know that I am God" (Psalm 46:10). Read that again: Be still. I am God. Period. You don't fix the problem; you don't fret about the problem; you just be still. He promises that, "In repentance and rest is your salvation, in quietness and trust is your strength" (Isaiah 30:15). This being still is not inaction; rather it is the best action. It is a trust in God's action opposed to my own action. All my actions summed up will leave me crying just like Kate, hanging on tightly with white knuckles and refusing to let go. If I would open that fist, God could give me the gift He is trying to. God looks down on me and says, "Be still, relax your grip, and open your hand to receive."

"The Lord will fight for you; you need only to be still."
Exodus 14:13

God, we fight and struggle for control over everything in our lives, including you. Teach us to be still, and you will give us rest. Life with you is filled with peace and you designed us to know that peace and walk in it. All we have to do is be still before you and choose it. Help us choose it. Help us to seek peace and pursue it. We pray that the peace of Christ would rule in our hearts. If we pay attention God, to your commands, you have promised peace like a river.

DAY 3
Reflux

Both of my children as infants were diagnosed with acid reflux. For those of you who have never experienced this, reflux is now what they used to call colic. Every parent who has ever had a child with this condition just felt my pain. It is hard to deal with any chronic problem that has no real solution. I remember after our first child, Kate, was born I was so tired because she *never* slept for more than fifteen minutes at a time. And she would be so tired that she would wake up screaming because when I laid her down the acid would come up. People used to say, "Sweetheart, you look so tired; you are supposed to sleep while *they* sleep." I wanted secretly to punch their lights out and say, "Are you listening to me; she doesn't sleep!"

Brian, my youngest child, was not born with this condition. He was a normal baby for the first three weeks, and my husband and I thought we were in heaven. Then he started developing Kate's symptoms. Meanwhile, I told God it wasn't fair. If he was going to let Brian have acid reflux too, he should have had it from the get go. That way we wouldn't know what we were missing. This was cruel and unusual punishment! God listened, and then I am pretty sure he chuckled at me.

One of the suggested treatments for acid reflux is to elevate the baby at all times, especially after eating and while sleeping. They need to be elevated for at least twenty minutes for the milk to begin to digest. I have yet to figure out the sleeping. If you elevate the crib mattress to a forty-five degree angle, as suggested, you end up with baby on their head at the bottom of the crib. Since these days you can't even let the babies sleep on their stomachs, I was thinking that a heap at the bottom of the crib is not okay. Aside from Velcro pajamas, which I have a patent pending on, I have no idea how this can actually work.

This made me think, if milk takes at least twenty minutes to digest, then what about God's word. Jesus is the "bread of life" and Jesus is the Word (John 6:35). Once read it has the habit of coming back up once or twice. Unless it is digested, it brings no nourishment. We often don't take the time and effort to spend twenty minutes of elevation so that we keep God's word down. There is so much to digest that we take an all or nothing approach. We attack our devotions needing to finish our three chapters for the day, and never get the nourishment we needed from the one verse God sent to our heart, the one we sped through. Don't get me wrong reading it is great, but if we want it to stick to our ribs we have to re-read, memorize, and breathe it. This approach takes time, and we are in a got-to-have-it-now society. We aren't willing to take the time needed. I mean come on; we have to have the psalms totally memorized by the end of the week if we want to stay on our schedule.

Verses that you have taken time to digest stick to your ribs, they can be revisited whenever needed, and it is needed in our lives to fight temptation. God's word needs to become part of who you are. It fuels your actions just like food fuels your body's action. When digested, it fortifies your bones. Much milk makes bones that aren't easily broken, but you have to keep it in long enough to swallow it, even when it's hard to swallow. There is nothing more powerful than the word of God. It is unlike any other word; in it is the power for living the life we are called to live.

I challenge you to start out by reading less, and meditating on more. Memorize a verse that you feel is just for you. Everybody has time for this; we just don't want to do it. I post my verses in the bathroom where I brush my teeth. I even have some posted beside the toilet. I am in there several times a day; why not do something useful? I can have a verse memorized in a few days just by reading it there. As most of you moms know, I am never actually in that room alone, so I read the scripture to my children while I go (and I mean in the children's sense of got to go). This works great because it distracts Brian, who was the epitome of terrible two, from grabbing the end of the toilet paper and running full speed out of the bathroom.

The more mature you become the more food you will need, and pretty soon you can add solid food to your diet. Then you really start to grow. "In fact, though by this time you ought to be teachers, you need someone to teach you the elementary truths of God's word all over again. You need milk, not solid food! Anyone who lives on milk, being still an infant, is not acquainted with the teaching about righteousness. But solid food is for the mature, who by constant use have trained themselves to distinguish good from evil" (Hebrews 5:12-14). It is time to step up and ask for at least finger foods. We live in a world where it becomes harder and harder to distinguish good from evil. I need to know and choose the good, and I can't learn that if I am not digesting scripture. The Bible itself is what you need. Devotionals are great, books and the experiences of others are wonderful aides, but there is only one inspired word. It is the solid food we need. Teachers and preachers are great, but we cannot stand on what they believe alone. We must be able to stand up and know what we believe for ourselves. We have to *know* the truth. You cannot do that without study. I am not saying don't use commentaries or devotionals, I am saying make sure you are memorizing and meditating on scripture everyday. Surround yourself with it until it becomes your reality. We must be able to catch that evil creeping into our daily lives because we are so used to the Truth that the contrast is unmistakable.

"And you will know the truth, and the truth will set you free."
John 8:32

O Father, give me a hunger and a thirst for you like nothing else. I pray that you would make me crave solid food. Help me as I digest your words. Let them become fortifying to my spirit. Let them make my spiritual bones strong so that I can accomplish more for you, and not be so easily broken.

DAY 4
Run like a Naked Two Year Old

"Therefore, since we are surrounded by so great a cloud of witnesses, let us lay aside every weight, and sin which clings so closely, and let us run with endurance, the race that is set before us" (Hebrews 12:1). I always had a problem with this scripture because I thought it didn't relate to me on a personal level. You see I used to teach aerobics, and I LOVE to exercise. I just don't understand running. Several people have asked me to run with them, and my response is always the same, I don't run unless someone is chasing me. Running seems so much like punishment to me, especially if it is done on a treadmill. However, I don't think this was the kind of running that the apostle Paul meant. One night after bath time, God gave me great clarity about this passage. Paul meant running with full abandon like a naked toddler who is excited that people are watching and wants everyone to chase them. I literally live out this visual aid every night. There is something about a naked toddler that makes them faster, and they know it. My two children can consistently outrun me when naked. Maybe it has something to do with the aerodynamics.

We are to run this race Paul talks about not just focused on the prize, but aware of that prize. We are to run like a naked two year old, with full abandon, never forgetting who we are running to. We have to learn to be caught up in the joy that lies before us. We are to run for the joy of running. I have never seen a naked child run, when it wasn't accompanied by insane amounts of giggling, and it isn't just them. Everyone in a two mile radius joins in their glee. This is exactly how we are to look at our run, our life as Christians.

Sometimes in the midst of life we miss the sheer joy of the run. We forget that Jesus and heaven is our prize. He is awaiting us at the end! Instead of taking life and making it an un-ending task list, we should be waving our arms and laughing, while enticing others to join us because we know where we are going. We run not to be the first to the finish line, but to enjoy the race and engage as many bystanders as possible with us. Every step brings us closer to Jesus and we are able to see more of Him as He watches us. That is the whole point! It never matters who gets there first. This doesn't mean we are not to be diligent. Have you seen the determination of a naked, dancing toddler who doesn't want to call it quits and put on her pajamas? That is how I want to go out, with God chasing me while I scream one more lap! So often I miss this, and I look at my run as a series of mile markers that are simply to be passed. God is not about drudgery. The race is great because we know the end! The finish line is filled with those who have gone before and are cheering us on. "We are surrounded by so great a cloud of witnesses" (Hebrews 12:1a). The Message puts it like this, "It means we'd better get on with it, strip down, start running and never quit! No extra spiritual fat, no parasitic sins." See, both translations indicate the naked toddler method. We have to strip down and get rid of anything that hinders us. What hinders you? What keeps you from total abandon? Is it others expectations? Is it unbelief? Strip it off. No matter what it is, it ties you to this earth and makes the run hard. Different things hinder us all, but what they are doesn't matter. The common denominator is that we don't need them.

When we get to that finish line, if we arrive totally defeated, alone and out of breath, we missed the point. Somewhere we have lost the joy of running for the love and exhilaration of pleasing Jesus. Children understand how to live in their moments. They understand how to let go of expectations, past failures and be in the now. That is the secret to the run. We throw off the pain from yesterday and we lay down the anxieties for tomorrow beside it. We know where we are headed and who is waiting. Why not enjoy the thrill of the wind in our face, the air in our lungs and entice as many people with us as we can possibly grab on the way.

"Therefore, since we are surrounded by so great a cloud of witnesses, let us lay aside every weight, and sin which clings so closely, and let us run with endurance, the race that is set before us."
Hebrews 12:1

God renew us so that we are fresh for the run. Make our feet swift and clear our path of obstacles no matter in what form they appear. Discipline us for the long distance, and let us take joy in each step. Give us the joy we should have so that others may see the difference! Let us strip down and get rid of the distractions of this world that slow us. Quite frankly, there isn't time for them, and they just hinder us from getting to the prize. Help us remember where we are headed without missing the joy of the journey and the lessons we need. Keep our focus on the finish so that the distractions of this world cannot pull us away.

DAY 5
It's MINE!

It's mine! Who teaches us this catchy phrase? I don't remember trying to repeat that phrase for Kate to mimic. I would love to blame it on her father, but I don't have any evidence. She seemed to learn that phrase of her own accord, and the idea of it came way before she could voice the opinion. She learned early to hold onto things Mommy was trying to take. If Mama wanted it, surely she should try to keep it for herself. She believed that obviously Mama is out to get her and deprive her of some joy. Surely there is nothing harmful about playing with the toilet brush and licking water from the dog's bowl. My son, Brian, has taken it a step farther, or maybe at sixteen months, he is just stronger than me already. When you take something from him, he likes to grab you with his other arm and try to bite you while you wrestle him for whatever his death grip is surrounding. With both children, the common theme is, "It's Mine!"

Ingrained into us is the idea that we really can't trust God. It is part of our heritage, passed down in the curse from the garden. Why can't I have that apple; God must be holding out on me. Satan was the original author of this idea. He hasn't needed to change this tactic. It seems to still be working quite well. If God is taking something from us, it must be something we should hold onto. It must be something fun that I am entitled to. In actuality God has never taken anything from me that I needed. He never snatches things from me. He gently asks; though I admit He can be persistent at times.

My biggest area of selfish indulgence is my time, the time I call "my time." I like it. It is so hard for me to give up, even though every time I give God my time He multiplies it for me. I mean this literally. It is almost like He allows me to get more accomplished in a shorter amount of time; He lines things up so they work out just right, and even delivers help when I need it. So why am I so reluctant to give Him my time? I know those of you who are mothers are screaming, "What time? I have *NO* time!" I know this seems offensive, but that is flesh crying out that this is truth. If this is offensive, the reason is because you know God wants more from you. He is a God of relationship. He wants to make your everyday life Holy because taking the time to meet with Him puts you on Holy Ground and brings Him into your everyday life. Everything He wants to accomplish in you takes time in His presence. Only that time can prepare you for whatever He might ask you to do.

I try to give God what I call the first fruits of my time. I go to him FIRST with the minutes I have been given. I spend my time with Him as soon as I get it. I do not do dishes, exercise, or pass go and collect two-hundred dollars until I meet with Him first! This idea changes everything. I am not giving Him my leftovers. He knows how big a deal this is to me. I cannot stress this enough. Please understand, this is not meant to make you feel guilt. That is an emotion I am totally familiar with and vehemently hate! It is not of God. He has blessed me time and time again through this thing we call motherhood; but it can be excruciatingly hard! I am writing to you as one who understands. As I write, I have two children under the age of four. I speak as one who feels the same things you do. I want you to understand what I have learned, if you honor God with what you have, He gives back so much more. He understands exactly what you have, be it time, resources, talent, whatever; He gave it to you. The best thing about God is that He doesn't demand it back. He waits patiently until we want to give it. It gives Him joy when we give out of a heart full of love. He knows how much I treasure my time that is what makes the gift special. When I give him the first fruits of my time, I am telling God that He is worth my best.

I heard someone once say, you have time for what you make time for. It may be trite, but its truth cannot be denied. If I look at my day, I make time for other things so how can I not make time for what is most important. I need it. I can't be made into a new person capable of dealing with whining, dirty diapers, time-outs, unending cleaning, runaway dogs, scrapes and bruises, and repetitive questions (just to name a few from the last ten minutes), unless I spend time with the one who enables me to be patient and kind, not envious or boastful, not self-seeking, not easily angered, and not keeping record of wrongs (1 Corinthians 13).

Whatever it is that can't be given up for time with God, it isn't worth it. No matter how you rationalize, it cannot be better. Not only can it not be better, it cannot replace the best. "Martha, Martha,' the Lord answered, 'You are worried and upset about many things, but only one thing is needed. Mary has chosen what is better and it will not be taken from her" (Luke 10:41). Mary chose what was best by sitting at the Lord's feet while Martha was concerned with good things, but not the best. I wonder how many times God has come to me to relieve me of the "toilet brush" I am clinging to and to give me something truly precious while I scream "Mine!" and hold on for dear life. If we choose what is best, there is no need to scream "Mine!" because *it cannot be taken from us.*

"Look carefully then how you walk,
not as unwise but as wise,
making the best use of the time,
because the days are evil."
Ephesians 5:15&16

I am reminded, as was David, in Psalm 31 that my times are in your hands. They are not in my hands. As much as I strive to hold onto it, time does not belong to me. Help me to choose to honor you with my time. Thank you that you are not at all limited by time. Remind me that my time here is like a vapor. Only time spent on you will last, everything else will vanish.

DAY 6
Heritage

I was at work one day when one of my colleagues, Kristie, remarked that she thought my children looked like me. Miss Lynn, another colleague standing with us, laughed out loud and then asked if Kristie knew my husband. When she replied no, that she had never met Pete, Miss Lynn said, "Well that explains it." You see my children look nothing like me. They are carbon copies of their father. My pastor's wife has often remarked that Kate is me trapped in Pete's body, although she acts like me, neither one looks at all like me.

Okay, so by now you know my children a little. I love them both dearly, but they could not be more different. They are like night and day! The question occurred to me, how can I love them both equally and so much at the same time? My daughter is one of the most lovable beings ever made. She is sweet and genuinely loving. She is also incredibly sensitive. My son, well my son is all boy. He is totally different. He is completely his father. I have never seen a child resemble a parent more. I mean they have the same flat spot on the back of their left ears. It's almost creepy. He reacts the same way that Pete does and they even find the same things funny. There is something about that which endears him to me. It's like an extension of the love I feel for his father. He is a living, breathing reminder of that love.

The other day, while I was reading Romans, I was struck with the thought that God's love for us is exactly like my love for my son. It discusses the remnant of Israel and how, in God's gracious provision, they are broken off of the vine until the fullness of the Gentiles has been attained (Romans 11:20&25). Paul goes on to explain that we should not in anyway take pride in this. "As regards the gospel, they are enemies for your sake. But as regards election, they are beloved for the sake of their forefathers" (v.28). Israel holds a special place in God's heart. They are beloved for the sake of their forefathers. Those forefathers: Abraham, Isaac, and Jacob, that God loved so dearly. All of Israel came from them. When God looks at Israel, just like when I look at Brian, He sees their fathers. The resemblance is dear to Him. They are His chosen ones.

Now for you and me this also holds true. We are the vine grafted in. We are graced with being a part of Israel by adoption (Romans 8:15 & Galatians 4:5). So when God looks at us, it is not with less love. You see when we became sons we didn't take on the nature of Israel, we took on the nature and body of Christ, His one and only son (Romans 5:1). When He looks at us, He sees Jesus. If we are united to Christ, we are dearly loved just as He is. That is a family resemblance like no other. When God looks at us, He loves us because in Jesus we are His children and joint heirs with Christ (Romans 8:17).

I long for it to be said of me that I look like Jesus. I also long for that heritage for my children. King David was a man after Gods own heart and scripture records the amazing amount of mercy bestowed on his children because of God's love for David. That one man, in all his sin, was the beloved of God. The decisions we make in our life will not just affect us, they affect our children and our children's children. Hebrews chapter 11 is often called the scriptural Faith "Hall of Fame". It records a beautiful picture of spiritual heritage, "By faith Isaac invoked future blessings on Jacob and Esau. By faith Jacob, when dying, blessed each of the sons of Joseph, bowing in worship over the head of his staff" (v.20&21). These men understood the link between prayer and blessings. They had faith in God and they faithfully trusted that their children had a place in their spiritual lineage. They knew that their actions had consequences on their children for their good or their harm.

Our heritage in Christ is a beautiful gift, and as parents we have a responsibility to teach them. By faith and because of my standing in Christ I want to invoke future blessings on them. I want God to recognize them because of their spiritual heritage. When God looks at Brian and sees the resemblance to Pete that He created, I pray He will one day also see His own son Jesus.

"And if children, then heirs–heirs of God and fellow heirs with Christ, provided we suffer with Him in order that we may also be glorified with Him."
Romans 8:17

Father, help us to better understand and value our heritage, not just spiritual heritage from our earthly fathers, but more importantly the beautiful heritage we have in Jesus. Help us to see this great gift of adoption and let it compel us to love. Help us to remember who we represent and who we want to resemble. Let us have faith too invoke future blessings on our children by our life and our prayers. Thank you that all of this happens because of your power and your plan. Thank you for the gift of being a joint heir with Christ though I cannot even fully comprehend this. Thank you that by your doing, when you look at me you don't see all my sin, you see Jesus.

DAY 7
Repeatedly Ruffled

Trust is a funny thing. I remember the first night that I "trusted" my husband to feed our baby girl while I got a little extra sleep. After the twelve times I asked if he was sure he burped her, he finally said, "Would you like to feed her, and *I will sleep*?" He was so right; he usually is. It is one of his more annoying qualities. See I want the extra rest, but am unwilling to let go of the control. It isn't that I don't trust my husband; I do. I want the baby fed, but I want her fed the way I would do it. I don't trust him to do things *my* way. Bless my husband's heart. It's no wonder he doesn't vacuum; he knows I would do it again right behind him.

I wonder if God, like my husband, ever wants to ask me if I would like to take over while *He* sleeps. Sometimes He must just look at me and say, "Oh the peace and rest you miss. I would give it to you, if you would just let go." Oh the amount of contentment and rest God offers that we just can't get our brains around. I am sometimes contented with so little if I could only have eyes to see the abundance God has for me. C.S. Lewis says, "We are half-hearted creatures, fooling about with drink and sex and ambition when infinite joy is offered us, like an ignorant child who wants to go on making mud pies in a slum because he cannot imagine what is meant by the offer of a holiday at the sea. We are far too easily pleased." He is right. I am so half-hearted. I am

22

content with far too little. Peace is available to us…real peace. Rest! Our lives could have rest everyday, apart from circumstances. Jesus holds this out to us and we turn and tell Him we like our way better. He offers what we cannot attain on our own and we know it. We still wander through our days with thoughts of clothes, food, and generally all sorts of things that won't matter tomorrow. If we would only let go, today would hold so much more value and we could enjoy the present without striving to control the future.

All of us women have struggled with this same issue. I know because I have talked to so many. In truth, the excessive vacuuming to perfection may not apply to all, but we all have our areas. We want the control because if we are honest, we are not sure we will like God's plans. What if ours are better? There it is; I said it. It's what we all think so often. That leads me to my point, (you thought I was never getting to it, I know). God is good. I have to say, as true as that statement is, it never brought me much comfort. Don't get me wrong; I am thankful God is good. It is one of His greatest points. It doesn't comfort me because quite frankly I rarely want what is good for me. Knowing that Broccoli is better for me than mint chocolate chip ice cream, doesn't make me want it. Paul says, "And we know that for those who love God all things work together for good, for those who are called according to his purpose" (Romans 8:28). Here are the key words in that verse, "HIS purpose" and "good". God doesn't work out my purposes for good; He works out His purposes. The way you define that second word makes all the difference. When He is working out these purposes, we have to remember that it is for our good. It's not for our rest, our own way, our list of desires, or even our agenda. It's for our good. Pete may not do things exactly the way I do, but his help is for my good and my rest. If I don't accept it, I will not receive the rest I need.

So again the question, "Knowing he is good, do we trust him?" Sometimes the problem is that we don't trust him to do it our way (a theme for me, apparently). Quite frankly I know my way isn't good enough, but I often fear His way. It gets me all out of control, and that seems to be just how He likes us. He has never let us down, not once. He has never left us. How can we not trust him? We often assume as soon as we say we trust Him that doubt goes away. That isn't how it works. You don't trust a person in a day, it takes time. Just because God is more trustworthy than people doesn't change the process. We often assume we are failures because we don't immediately become peaceful and tranquil creatures whose feathers are never ruffled. If you are seeking God, expect to be radically ruffled, repeatedly. It reminds me of shampoo, you know lather, rinse, and repeat. It's the same kind of cycle. I will get ruffled and God will smooth; I will get ruffled and God will remind me that he doesn't need my help; I just need to rest in his presence. Then I will get ruffled and maybe this time I smooth more quickly because the last time I listened to God and rested, and I remember Him. I will again get ruffled but with practice I remember Him, and I rest. He is for my good. It isn't always comfortable, but if we will believe Him and let Him, He will always smooth our feathers and give us peace. We believe him by assuring ourselves that whatever is happening it's not out of His control. Repeating what the bible says about this helps. Then we must let go of our illusion of control and repeatedly, as many times as it takes, give Him back the steering wheel. This last act works best from our knees because it reminds us of whom we are and Who He Is!

"For we share in Christ, if indeed we hold our original confidence to the end" (Hebrews 3:14). This verse implies that we are missing out if we do not hold our original confidence to the end. That doesn't mean we don't ever have a moment of doubt. If your life is like mine, there is much time spent in fearful anticipation. We have to learn where to take that. We take it to a God who has a purpose for our good and we rest it there come what may. Again, lather, rinse, repeat or rather; kneel, pray, and repeat.

"And we know that for those who love God all things work together for good, for those who are called according to his purpose."
Romans 8:28

O Father, help us as we try so hard to let go. The world is a scary place, as you well know. You didn't intend it to get this way, but thanks to us it did. Thank you that you didn't just leave us here. Thank you that as many times as it takes, you will keep perfecting us. Even when we tire of the process, you don't. Even when we doubt our victory over sin, you don't; because you have seen Jesus in us. When you look at us, you see him. Help us to cry out with the Father in Mark 9:24, "I do believe, help my unbelief!" Thank you that you are here as long as it takes, which most assuredly will be until the day we come home. You are for our good in a place where there are few promises like that. Help us to desire your good.

DAY 8
I wanna hold your Hand! (Not the Beatles version)

When our daughter Kate really walked for the first time, she was ten months old. No hanging on, no counting three or four steps, she just started walking. Then she was running. She was very sure that nothing can get in her way. I am pretty sure that she thinks if she ran hard enough, she might be able to get through the wall. She has tried repeatedly. She didn't want my hand anymore because she was sure she didn't need it. Her enthusiasm was not limited by her actual ability. In her tiny little world she had decided that the laws of physics did not apply to her. She didn't get that the one thing keeping her from certain injury was my hand, which had become the bane of her existence.

"For I, the Lord your God, hold your right hand; it is I who say to you 'Fear not, I am the one who helps you'" (Isaiah 41:13). I am thankful that when we run headlong away from Him, sure that we know where we are going, He is steady and keeps us from certain disaster. He does not let go of our hand. No matter how much we squirm and whine and try to pull away. When we act like children running from their mothers, He is patient and stands steady. He will not let us go. He does not yank us back or yell. He simply holds tightly and waits for us to finish our tantrums. Sometimes I wonder how God waits that long with such patience.

God is diligent in His discipline of those He loves. He is not moved by our whines and He does not bend to our whims. That is such a comfort to me. When I get ahead of myself, He is not going to let me run headlong into disaster to spare my feelings. He knows better than me. Sometimes I fight against Him, sometimes I scream against Him, but He is unmoving. Like a good parent He can take it. He knows who He is. He is big enough to take our emotion and He doesn't let it sway His decisions.

I know it is hard to be excited about discipline. However, we should understand that we are disciplined because of our position. God only disciplines those He loves (Proverbs 3:12). God says, "It is for discipline that you have to endure. God is treating you as sons. For what son is there whom his father does not discipline? If you are left without discipline, in which all have participated, then you are illegitimate children and not sons" (Hebrews 12:7&8). God disciplines us as sons. It is out of love. He is preparing us for Heaven. He doesn't do it to see us in pain or to make life harder. "For the moment all discipline seems painful rather than pleasant, but later it yields the peaceful fruit of righteousness to those who have been trained by it" (v. 11). He disciplines us to bring us the peaceful fruit of righteousness. We are His legitimate children and joint heirs with Christ. "And if children, then heirs—heirs of God and fellow heirs with Christ, provided we suffer with him in order that we may also be glorified with him" (Romans 8:17). We are joint heirs with Christ! Seriously, that is the best news I have heard in a lifetime. We are made out of dust, but God is going to make us into His heir.

God has to discipline me because like Kate, my enthusiasm is greater than my actual ability. He keeps me from certain harm, and He uses discipline to do it. He does this so that we can be a part of His family. He is making us an heir with Christ.

> "If you think of this world as a place intended simply for our
> happiness, you find it quite intolerable; think of it as place for
> correction and it's not so bad."
> –C.S. Lewis

"For I, the Lord your God, hold your right hand; it is I who say to you
'Fear not, I am the one who helps you.'"
Isaiah 41:13

God I pray that you give wisdom to identify the feel of your hand holding me back. Thank you that you keep me from sudden disasters that I know nothing about. The next time I get ready to throw a fit, help me remember that I am a child. I don't know everything, and I am not able to do things by myself; as much as I may pretend to. Thank you for your gentle pressure, applied to my life when I get ready to run headlong into the wall. Redirect my enthusiasm when it threatens to overtake wisdom.

DAY 9
Taking a Time Out

Time-out has always been hilarious at our house. Brian has caught on to the idea of how it works. He has seen Kate being sent to time out. He has not yet been sent to time-out for his own crime, but anytime that he can get his hands on Kate's time out mat; he runs into the kitchen, puts the mat in the middle of the floor, and throws himself headlong into a fit of crying. He feels the need to imitate his sister. He has somewhere missed the point, but clearly knows the motions.

Once when Kate was sent to time out, she did something to Brian, though I can't remember what...dropped him on his head maybe? Anyway, amidst all the weeping and gnashing of teeth, she plops down on her mat screaming only to be sat on by Brian, still screaming at the top of his lungs. He refuses to move; he is blocking my way to her on purpose. She throws her arms around him and hangs on for dear life and there the two of them sit...still screaming. Never mind that he is the offended party. He doesn't want her punished. He will cry until she stops crying, and so it goes. It would be beautiful if it wasn't so darn infuriating.

Brian's grand gesture is genuine love. It is beautiful because it is a picture of what we are supposed to do and feel. We are supposed to be distressed by others pain and need for God to the point that we want to stand in the gap for them, even when they are being punished for a crime that they committed against us, like Brian. We are to go in front of them and say "Have Mercy!" Anybody ever done that? Ever prayed for mercy from God for someone who has hurt you? We are called to, and I have never obeyed that particular call with zeal and passion. I have never prayed with tears of compassion that an offender be spared punishment. Oh but I have prayed, in tears, for myself to be spared. Why the double standard? Of course everyone deserves the same amount of mercy. It is easy to agree that that is true, but hard to apply to my persecutors. Why pray for mercy on ourselves and neglect the prayer for others?

Children have a clearer picture. They have not yet learned to steep in selfishness. They forgive more easily. Maybe it's because they have a shorter memory. Maybe we should pray for shorter memories to be extended to us. That may sound crazy to those of you like me who have trouble remembering where I put the keys, grocery list, shoes, or what I was just saying. I seem to loose memory capacity more each day, but I have no trouble remembering the name of the kid who picked on me on the bus, or the day I got in trouble for something I didn't do. I can recall those memories with vivid detail. I have nursed them in my mind until they are treasures of sorts. Those aren't the kind of treasures we are to store away. Each of us has them though. It's time to let them go and pray for the offenders, not just out of duty, but out of love. If you have none to give, go to the one who does. He is faithful to answer our prayers, especially when they are in line with His will for our obedience. He will provide the love. The more you practice the prayer the more love you will find. One day you will find that suddenly you mean it, you feel compassion for those who have hurt you. That is a return to love.

Take a time out today on your mat and pray for someone who has hurt and offended you. Ask God to make you genuine and give you love. That is a prayer He runs to answer. "For if you forgive men when they sin against you, your heavenly Father will also forgive you. But if you do not forgive men their sins, your Father will not forgive your sins" (Matthew 6: 14&15). We have been forgiven so much. How can we not plead for the forgiveness of others?

"If I speak in the tongues of men and angels, but have not love,
I am only a resounding gong or a clanging cymbal.
If I have the gift of prophecy
and can fathom all mysteries and all knowledge,
and if I have faith that can move mountains, but have not love,
I am nothing. If I give all I posses to the poor and surrender my body
to the flames,
but have not love, I gain nothing."
1 Corinthians 13:1-3

God make me weep for those who have hurt me. Remind me that those who hurt have first been hurt. Give me a forgiving heart so that I can be forgiven. Overwhelm me with love so that I can't help but spill it onto others. Make me different than the world, because they will know me by my love. Teach me to intercede for others, not just those who are easy to love, but those who are difficult. Let my prayers eventually be a reflection of the love I feel for those who have hurt me.

Another arrival occupies my thoughts today. As much as I love to be the first to catch the glimpse of Daddy's truck, I am thinking more of the arrival of my Heavenly Father. He is coming back. I forget it so often that when I actually think about it, it is surprising. How much sweeter would it be on Jesus' arrival day if I was one of the first to catch a glance of Him because I was looking up? How I would love to yell at the top of my lungs, "Daddy's here!" on that day. Sadly, I am often too occupied with the things of this world to look up. My thoughts are occupied with the here and the temporal. The reason Kate sees her daddy first is that she is singular in purpose. She is not distracted. Her faith guides her actions. I rarely remind myself in the morning that today could be the day my father comes home. I don't think about Jesus coming back as a possible event in my lifetime. Do you? It is not that I don't believe it will happen; it's that I don't think I will still be here to see it. I think if most of us are honest, this is how we feel too. "In the last days…they will say; "Where is this 'coming' he promised? Ever since our fathers died, everything goes on as it has since the beginning of creation. But they *deliberately forget* that long ago by god's word the heavens existed and the earth was formed…" (2 Peter 3:4&5, emphasis mine). I don't want to be found deliberately forgetting. I must then deliberately remember. We have to remember that the word of God has a splendid history of being fulfilled. If he says it will happen, it happens!!! " So Christ, having been offered once to bear the sins of many, will appear a second time, not to deal with sin to save those who are eagerly waiting for him" (Hebrews 9:28). How does one "eagerly wait, by preparing our hearts? Peter instructs us, "…what kind of people ought you to be? You ought to live holy and godly lives as you look forward to the day of God and speed its coming" (2 Peter 3:11b&12a). He goes on to say, " so then dear friends, since you are looking forward to this, make every effort to be found spotless, blameless, and at peace with him" (v.14).

If you are expecting someone, you make every effort to be ready. You talk about it to your family and everyone else who is waiting. We are to be doing just this with the body of Christ. "Let us hold fast the confession of our hope without wavering, for he who promised is faithful. And let us consider how to stir up one another to love and good works, not neglecting to meet together, as is the habit of some, but encouraging one another, and all the more as you see the day drawing near" (Hebrews 10:23-25).

I know that the earliest Christians saw Jesus in person. They expected Him because they had seen Him leave. His coming back was more real to them. But with the passage of more and more time, it becomes increasingly more likely that He will return soon. Each day we live brings us one day closer. Isn't that an amazing thought? If we live as if this is a reality, we will not be disappointed. If Jesus still hasn't come back by our dying day, we will still be with Him momentarily; so we have nothing to loose.

From the time Kate wakes up, Daddy coming home is her focus. I would love that to be said of me. From the time my feet hit the floor in the morning, I am expecting Him. I want to look for Jesus around every corner. I know in my head that when God is done with His work, He is coming for us as fast as He can, but I want to train my heart to expect him. If we expect him any minute we will live with more urgency. If a toddler can have that kind of focus waiting for her Daddy, then surely we can have a better focus waiting for ours. We need to practice reading the signs and looking out the window. We need to expect with joy that it could be the next hour. When He comes I want to be found looking up. Our expectations should not settle on earth but ascend to the power of Heaven.

"Let us hold fast the confession of our hope without wavering,
for he who promised is faithful."
Hebrews 10:23

Father, I know that for the time being you are out of my sight. Teach me to long for the sight of you. Help me to let go of this world. Bit by bit until I am consumed by the thought that you are near, and that one day soon this will all fade away and I will have what I long for. In a moment the temporal will fade into the eternal. Help me to practice seeing with eternal eyes that are fixed on you and erase our doubt. Give my faith an element of expectation. Thank you that I can know you as a God who will never fail to meet my expectations.

DAY 11
Strapped to the Truth

I delight myself in telling you this next story. Though I could be taken as a girly girl, I have another side. It's almost like a secret life of adventure. I have my own four-wheeler, a gift from my husband. I love telling people that I have my own four-wheeler! They get the best look on their faces. My husband is such a good influence on me; he enables me to be so much more fun than I actually am. Anyway, when Kate was little we rode often. Lest you turn me in for child abuse, you should know we have a riding contraption, which straps her to me in case of an accident. This device, though lacking in fashion, is very safe and functional.

Kate loved to try and reach the handlebars. It must have given her the illusion that she was in control of our destiny. What she would do with them if attained, I can only dare to guess, but it was a comical procedure to watch as she strained against, well… her restraints. You and I know they are for her protection; she was sure they were for her annoyance. I was struck with the idea that she didn't like being unable to control where we were headed. I identified. After a short time, she realized that she was perfectly content to lean back on me and ride. With the wind in her hair, she began to wave her arms in a dance over her head. This is standard procedure for her rides. She also liked to sing wordless tunes and dance (she gets this preoccupation with herself from her mother; it comes also with delusions of grandeur). She was perfectly happy until we finished our ride and arrived back in our yard where I regret having taught her sign language, as she incessantly gestured for more…more!!

I wish I could adapt as quickly as her. I wish I took being strapped to the Driver how it was intended; for my protection and peace. Everyday I choose whether I will reach for the illusion of driving or strap myself to the driver and enjoy the ride. To enjoy the ride, I have to continually remind myself who I am strapped to. Thankfully He left us an incredible tool for that.

There is actually a command in scripture for us to strap ourselves to the Truth. The word used is to bind. Bind is defined, by my dictionary concordance, as *to fasten or tie together* (NIV). These were the instructions for the Israelites, "These commandments that I give to you today are to be upon your hearts. Impress them on your children. Talk about them when you sit at home and when you walk along the road, when you lie down and when you get up. *Tie* them as symbols on your hands and bind them on your foreheads. Write them on the doorframes of your houses and on your gates" (Deuteronomy 6:6-9). And then again, "Keep my commands and you will live; guard my teachings as the apple of your eye. *Bind* them on our fingers; write them on the tablet of your heart" (Proverbs 7:2&3). We are to be so close to love and God's commands that we are to bind them to us, around our neck and on our fingers. If you had a reminder like this bound to your neck and your fingers all day, it would definitely affect you. Can you even imagine? It is easy to remember something when the reminder is EVERYWHERE. So where do we learn about love and God's commands? I know this will shock you but it's all in the Word, the Bible. "In the beginning was the Word, and the Word was with God, and the Word was God. He was with God in the beginning" (John 1:1). These words are divinely inspired and written down for us. Though we do not see Jesus face to face as John did, God left us the Word and the Holy Spirit. The Word was God so when we bind ourselves to the

Word, we are binding ourselves to the driver. He is the director of man's paths. "I know, O Lord, that a man's life is not his own; it is not for man to direct his steps" (Jeremiah 10:23).

When you are reluctant to trust the driver, when you doubt that what you are doing matters, when you are tired of doing things the way God wants, when you are just tired, you strap yourself to the Truth and you hang on. You bind that truth to you so that it is attached to you; it is always with you and before you. Some of you are thinking that I am speaking metaphorically; I assure you I am not. I have God's word on my walls, in my purse, on my desk, on my bathroom mirror, even beside my potty (for those of you without children I will use the adult word, toilet). It has to be everywhere I look until it becomes where I turn. Let me rephrase. It is like anything else that requires practice. You do it again and again until it becomes a habit. I take my fears and thoughts and questions to the Truth until the Truth becomes habit, and I know the verses without having to look them up. I can sit back and let God drive; I can enjoy the wind in my hair and sing, because I don't just *have* the Truth, I *know* the Truth.

"Many are the plans in a man's heart,
but it is the Lord's purpose that prevails."
Proverbs 19:21.

Help me learn to be content as I strap myself to you as you drive my life. Help me to consistently struggle less because I miss the singing and the wind in my hair when I do. Teach me the Truth until I know you and you are with me everywhere. Show me how to practice it. Give me peace that passes all understanding as I realize more and more that I am strapped to the driver of the Universe, who cares where we are headed?

DAY 12
Can You Hear Me Now?

Brian feels the need to repeat everything he says to make sure that he is clear. He also uses this tactic to stall when he is at a loss. "Because…because…because…because I need to." I should tell you that this works well for him because the way he actually sounds is adorable. His "because" actually comes out phonetically as "pecuz". My daughter Kate, on the other hand seems to constantly repeat words because she wants to make sure that she is being heard. "Mommy, mommy, Mommy, Mommy, umm, Mommy"…,"Yes darling", I patiently respond. Mommy, Mommy, Mommy, etc…, I answer, "Yes"… and then she replies, "I don't remember." A couple of minutes will pass and then, "Hey Mommy!" And it keeps up constant and unending.

Children tell stories in a roundabout way that involves repetition and painstaking attention to detail. I can identify because I never grew out of this stage. Sometimes, especially when Kate is trying to tell me something, it is literally all that I can do to listen. She wants my complete attention for a 15 minute story about the last time she fell, went to the bathroom, or brushed her teeth. Quite frankly, I love her but this is one of the hardest things I need to do for her – listen. I am working on making sure that I maintain eye contact for the duration of the story, and that I am engaged in it, no matter how uneventful, because it is important to her. This could one day kill me. Sometimes that child will take 5 minutes to find the right word, but I am learning not to supply them for her. This only serves to annoy her and make her forget her spot. It is excruciating to wait patiently even when I know what she is trying to say.

The psalmist requests of God, "incline your ear to me Rock of refuge to which I may continually come" (Psalm 71:2&3). I love how the message phrases it, "put your ear to the ground and listen...you said your door was always open." I love the picture of God with his ear pressed and listening, giving His complete attention.

Unlike my struggle with my children, God can bear the weight of all the things I have to say. Even when the weight of the words are too much for me, and I can't quite pick the right ones the spirit intercedes for me with groans too great for words. Unlike Kate, I realize I need the help. God knew that our language is limited; He provided for the times that I don't even have the words. God made provision for this with the Holy Spirit, "In the same way, the Spirit helps us in our weakness. We do not know what we ought to pray for, but the Spirit himself intercedes for us with groans that words cannot express" (Romans 8:26). When I can't find the words or simply don't even know what I really mean, I don't have to. It continues, "He who searches hearts knows what is the mind of the Spirit, because the Spirit intercedes for the saints according to the will of God" (v.27). God is able to search my heart and know its meaning. When I cannot make myself clear to anyone else, I am clear and understood to God. I have His complete understanding. This Holy Spirit God gave us is also a gift of memory. "He will teach you all things and bring to your remembrance all that I have said to you" (John 14:26). The Holy Spirit can remind us of the truth of God that we already know. He brings to remembrance the truth when it is needed for encouragement or instruction.

I take great comfort in knowing that we serve a personal God who gives personal attention to our prayers. When I take the time as a mother to get on Kate's level and look her in the eyes, she will sometimes stop repeating and stuttering. Though I sometimes lack patience to understand the heart of the matter, God never misunderstands us. He is always ready to put his ear to our level and He is willing to stop and make eye contact with us for as long as it takes, or just as long as we want. Don't miss that great gift because you feel that your prayers should be elegant and wordy. That prayer is not for God, but for man. Don't miss this gift because you think you need to be in the right place to pray. We are to pray continually, giving thanks. This seems like an insurmountable task until we realize that prayer is simply opening a direct line for us to be infused with the Spirit. When we pray, we acknowledge that we don't have an answer or more simply that God *is* the answer. "In all your ways acknowledge him, and he will direct your paths" (Proverbs 3:6). Prayer put simply is acknowledgement of God. It is giving thanks for who He is and what He does for us. He sustains us moment by moment. Constant prayer is moment by moment recognizing that He is there sustaining us. It is giving thanks. It is a refocusing of our gaze off of ourselves to something greater. When I stop to refocus on God, He holds my gaze. Each time I do, He holds my attention a little longer and a little longer and it becomes habit. Constant prayer is training the mind to think on God and not on this world. It releases us to see God instead of the illusion of control that we were holding. "Continue steadfastly in prayer, being watchful in it with thanksgiving" (Colossians 4:2). We are to be watchful in prayer with thanksgiving. Watch for ways to thank God, acknowledge that He sustains you. Watch for how He communicates to our hearts. Tune in and pay close attention. There is nothing more important. Prayer is thanking God that *He is*. Being steadfast in prayer releases us to live in faith minute by minute and rest. It allows us to rest because it affirms that we are not in control, but someone greater is. Children have a firm grasp on who is in control of their days. They may sometimes push for their own control, but they know where to go for help. They know that we as parents are there, and we will seek to understand them.

Prayer is reaching our hands to God and saying I am not big enough. I am not big enough to make sense of the world or even my day. Prayer is to be constant and unending, giving my thoughts to God and letting Him re-shape them. He reshapes them when I listen. I want my communication with God to be constant and unending. Even when it sounds like the unending and uneventful story of a child, the fact that I want to share it with Him is what makes it special. I know that He is patient and the more I talk the more He alters my words. Because He knows the thoughts and intentions of our heart, we can never be misunderstood. The next time my children come to me with a story or just a thought, I want to remember how patiently God listens to us.

"Continue steadfastly in prayer, being watchful in it with thanksgiving."
Colossians 4:2

Father I need you moment by moment. I try in my own efforts and I only fail. I thank you that you always listen, and that you can interpret my heart. Thank you for the gift of the Holy Spirit, who not only intercedes for me, but calls to mind the truth when I need it. Thank you that your presence with me is a gift whenever I draw near to you. Thank you that you give me this gift out of love for me. You want for me to experience life with you moment by moment and you intended peace for me. Thank you that Jesus died to give us that peace. When the world and all its cares threaten to sweep us away help us to hold steadfastly to you, the anchor for our souls (Hebrews 6:19). Thank you that there is never a time that you are too busy for us. You don't even sleep. We have complete access to you because of Jesus. Let us not take that for granted.

DAY 13
Who Was That Invisible Man?

I was recently in the car with a friend. We were not with our children but the conversation had drifted to them. She asked me what I tell my children when they are scared in the night, which inevitably all kids are. I ran through all the norms like; "There is nothing to be scared of because Jesus is always with you; even though you can't see Him, He is always here"; "Jesus can always see you because He can see everything"; and "There isn't anyone who is as big and strong as Jesus". To which she replied that these are the same things that she tells her son. However, his reaction caused me to laugh so hard I cried and nearly ran off the road. She said that he responded by screaming, "Get him out of here; I don't want him in here! Make him go away!"

The reason I found this hilarious is that it totally clicked for me where he was coming from. What two year old wants a guy who is incredibly strong and sees us all the time, while remaining invisible, lurking in his room? "Jesus is always there even when you can't see Him", makes sense to us as adults, but talk about scary. Never mind that you can't see Him, we also tell them that He is bigger and stronger than anything else. They don't need to get scared from watching TV; they have invisible, stronger than anyone giants in their own rooms who see everything!

The world says that we, as Christians, are crazy to believe in the invisible. God says that they have denied what has always been visible. Romans tells us that, "although they knew God, they did not honor Him as God or give thanks to Him, but they became futile in their thinking and their foolish hearts were darkened" (Romans 1:20). Because they do not honor God, they are in the dark; which can make it hard to see. When you are in the dark, the invisible is that much scarier. The world becomes futile in their thinking because they exchanged the truth about God for a lie. Why would anyone do that? We suppress the truth, and we do this by not honoring God or giving Him thanks. The world suppresses the truth and attributes everything to chance, and they remain in the dark. To see and acknowledge God would require change. Knowledge of God would impart responsibility to God. They, in turn, choose to stay in the dark.

Seeing the invisible is what we, as Christians, are called to. Hebrews states that Moses endured as seeing Him who is invisible. If we want to endure, we also have to see Him who is invisible. So how do we see Him and keep out of the dark? We honor God and give Him thanks (Romans 1:20). We acknowledge His work in our lives. Where the world says coincidence, we see the hand of God. His intent was for you to see Him in nature and all around, in everything He created. God's invisible qualities are all visible there. He is the invisible God because instead of seeing Him in everything, the world has seen only themselves.

When we choose to acknowledge Him and thank Him, then we begin to see Him everywhere because we see the working of His hand. Being thankful acknowledges that your circumstances come directly from God's hand. When you have acknowledged all the good that has come from His hand and have been thankful for it, you can take the seemingly bad from His hand too. Only because you have rehearsed all the past good, can you grasp that what might seem bad now, comes from the God who has given you so much good. You have established His character in your mind by rehearsing His faithfulness. Even then it is often scary, and there are times that you have to press your head against His chest and cover your other ear to drown out the world's voices so you can hear that beat of truth. You have to focus on it and refuse to believe other voices…"we destroy arguments and every lofty opinion raised against the knowledge of God, and take every thought captive to obey Christ" (2 Corinthians 10:5). You can be convinced without seeing. When you don't understand Him, you can know God is good because He has proven His character. That is how we endure, and see Him who is invisible. Rehearse His goodness and give thanks for everything given, honor and acknowledge that it is He who gives.

"For in this hope we were saved. Now hope that is seen is not hope. For who hopes for what he sees? But if we hope for what we do not see, we wait for it with patience" (Romans 8:24&25). Our hope is in what we cannot see. The comfort in an invisible God is that He holds invisible possibilities. He knows the solutions I can't see. Better yet He *is* the solution I can't see. I will rest in hope and wait with patience.

"For in this hope we were saved. Now hope that is seen is not hope. For who hopes for what he sees? But if we hope for what we do not see, we wait for it with patience." Romans 8:24&25

Father, help me to lean in and hear your heart beat. Teach me to honor you and thank you for all of your gifts. That is protection against the dark. Open my eyes to your attributes all around me. Give me a clear picture of your power for those who believe. Help me to focus on you so much that I see the unseen. Give me hope and patience to endure as one who sees the invisible. Help me to tear down arguments set up by the world to make me doubt you. Give me courage to see you even when I feel the dark. As I learn to acknowledge and thank you, grow my faith.

DAY 14
No Edge

Picture with me, if you will, a beautiful, Victorian bed. You know the kind; they have a set of steps beside them and appear in magazines and Bed and Breakfasts. You would never actually walk up those steps, unless you were three foot eight, but they look inviting. We recently acquired one of these beds from a friend, minus the staircase. My daughter was four months old at the time. She was on the afore mentioned Victorian bed, as I put away the laundry. As I stood right beside her, and I mean *right* beside her, Kate decided to see if she could fly. I have seen this whole scene played out multiple times in my recurring nightmares. You know those nightmares where you are falling and falling and you wake up right before you hit the ground. Same thing, but *she* is falling and falling, and it isn't a dream! She rolls, I can't catch her, and she cracks her head on our hardwood floor. (If you are a parent you know that sound. If you are not a parent, let me re-create if for you. It is the same thud a melon makes when it hits the floor). I scoop her up and proceed to panic, just following protocol for new mothers. I call the doctor, and they tell me to call 911. Let me say that at this point, that was just the encouragement I needed. It calmed me down tremendously. (Insert sarcasm!) She doesn't need a doctor; she needs an ambulance! I have broken the baby! My daughter is screaming; I am crying, and they are now sending an ambulance. To sum up: they arrive, check her out, and she is going to be fine. She stopped crying as soon as I stopped crying. She didn't even get much of a lump; I, on the other hand am scarred for life. I may still require medication.

Two days later, Kate was crawling on the same bed not missing a beat. She would rush to the edge certain that I would catch her, or that she could fly; I am not sure which. She had no recollection of teetering over the edge. In her mind, there was no edge. She had complete trust that there was nothing to worry about. I sat back fascinated, not for long mind you, the child is crazy!

How is this kind of trust possible? Does she have no memory? Did the initial fall cause serious brain damage? No, she is simply sure that everything in her world is fine. She is fresh; she doesn't understand that I am not all-powerful. It strikes me as odd that she is so new to the world, but she has something I can't seem to master. I serve an all powerful God, and I still can't seem to understand that I am perfectly safe. But she on the other hand has no fear. According to Psalm 121:3, my God is so vigilant that he doesn't even sleep. Kate has perfect trust in a fallible mother. God is asking me to live on the edge because He is infallible. This is what Jesus meant when he said; "I tell you the truth, unless you change and become like little children, you will never enter the kingdom of heaven" (Matthew 18:3). Unless I depend on God like a child, I will not know him. I must have confidence in not just his ability to fix the problem, but his decision of how. In the world, dependence on anyone or thing is a sign of immaturity but spiritually, dependence is a sign of the mature. If I can't get through one day, one hour, one minute without Jesus I am not weak, rather I display Jesus strength. I am putting on His life, His self and becoming like Christ as He lives in me. I have to seek everyday to forget the possibility of a fall and live like there is no edge. This doesn't mean I imagine the edge away, or that I don't believe it exists anymore. It means that I trust God in such a way that I choose not to remember the edge. Hour by hour and minute by minute, instead of focusing on the edge, I choose to focus on God. He knows where the edge is. He doesn't sleep. His gaze is always on us. Read that again, His gaze is ALWAYS on you.

This principle applied to life can make us do crazy illogical things, like Peter getting out of a boat and onto the water. Because of his obedience, he walked on water with Jesus. He focused on Jesus just long enough to achieve something impossible. Granted shortly thereafter he looked away and sank like a stone; the only reason he accomplished anything was because he gazed into the eyes of Jesus instead of seeing the waves around him. The world will absolutely think you are crazy, even other Christians will. They will say you are naïve, but God says the He will show them otherwise. "If the Lord delights in a man's way, he makes his steps firm; though he stumble, he will not fall, for the Lord upholds him with his hand" (Psalm 37:23&24). We cannot fail, even if we fall, because God upholds us.

"If the Lord delights in a man's way,
he makes his steps firm;
though he stumble,
he will not fall,
for the Lord upholds him with His hand."
Psalm 37:23&24

O God, give me a gaze that is straight into your eyes. Allow me to see you and not the edge. Grant me the assurance that you never take your gaze off of me. There is nowhere I can go that you are not present. I could not escape you if I wanted to. You hold me fast. Where can I go from your Spirit? Where can I flee from your presence? If I go up to the heavens you are there; if I make my bed in the depths you are there. If I rise on the wings of the dawn, if I settle on the far side of the sea, even there your hand will guide me; your right hand will hold me fast" (Psalm 139:7-10). With this knowledge, I pray that whatever act of obedience I am shrinking from, you will give me the courage to live like there is no edge.

DAY 15
Germs and Jesus

You know those people who feel it is a religious and moral directive not to touch anything in a public restroom. I am one of them. I wash my hands and use the paper towel to turn off the faucet and open the door, maneuvering with my knee or feet to keep it open while I balance to throw the towel away. I know, I know you wish you had my skill, but wait it gets better. At this stage in my life, I have perfected the hover. Never touching the toilet seat, I gracefully exit the restroom untarnished. With all of these accomplishments under my belt, I entered into a new realm of the germ challenge when my daughter started to potty train. To me it was the equivalent of another level in a video game. I had to pull out my A game. This sent me into a whole new arena of crazy maneuvers. Did you know they make stick-on toilet seat covers for toddlers? I tossed some in my buggy just the other day, delighted with my find, and my husband leaned over and said, "You know those aren't for adults."

Now this anecdote is not entirely about me. This next part was told to me by a friend, Nicolle. It is a story about her close friend. Apparently this woman reminds Nicolle of me; we both clean the inside of our trash cans regularly. Nicolle thought I was just the person to appreciate this doctor office drama.

Her friend feels about the doctor's office much like I feel about public restrooms. If you touch anything while there, you need to be dropped into a vat of sanitizer. When taking her three year old to the pediatrician, this lovely woman was paying at the window when she turned around to locate her son, and to her horror found that he had completely stuffed one of the waiting room toys into his mouth. Knowing that her son knew better than to touch the toys in the waiting room, she proceeded to shout, "What are you doing, don't you know how many germs are on that!" To which her son replied, "'Germs' and 'Jesus', that's all I ever hear, and I've never seen a one of 'em!"

I have the distinct feeling that my children will know clearly how I feel about germs. I act on my knowledge of them even though I personally have "never seen a one of 'em.'" My children know they will reap many sanitizing consequences from touching unauthorized objects. They may even adopt my feelings as they grow up. My question is this, will my children know without a doubt what I believe about Jesus. Will it be as apparent and clear as how I feel about germs? Will they hear about Him so much from me that they know He's real? Do I act on my knowledge of Jesus enough for my kids to pick up how I feel and adopt it? If I do not talk about Jesus everyday and make him part of my everyday life, then they won't. Unless they see me read my Bible everyday, I can't tell them how much it means to me. It will be a hollow argument. When I explain that when they have trouble or are scared that they should take it to Jesus, they won't unless they have seen me do it countless times. We all avoid the bad things we don't want our kids to pick up, like the words you didn't realize were naughty until someone repeated them, and suddenly they sound terrible. If we are diligent about the things we don't want them to imitate, why not be diligent about the ones we do. If you want your kids to have faith in Jesus, then it is time for you to upgrade to your A game. I want my children to be able to say they know God is real. Not because their mommy said He is, but because they have seen Him in my life. I want them to see that Jesus is more to me than anything else. They will learn that He is my everything, or they will learn that He is just someone I talk about. They will either learn that He has power to help in their time of need, or they will learn that He is powerless.

"These commandments that I give you today are to be upon your hearts. Impress them on your children. Talk about them when you sit at home and when you walk along the road, when you lie down and when you get up" (Deuteronomy 6:6&7). Make Jesus real to them. Talk about Him in the car, while you make dinner, while you shop, and everywhere you go. Let Him be the theme of your music, dinner conversation, and life. Your children won't miss it; they will imitate it.

"Train a child in the way he should go, and he will not depart from it."
Proverbs 22:6

"Write these commandments that I've given you today on your hearts. Get them inside of you and then get them inside your children. Talk about them wherever you are, sitting at home or walking in the street; talk about them from the time you get up in the morning to when you fall into bed at night."
Deuteronomy 6:6&7 *Message*

Father, I pray that you will be all my children have known from birth. I pray that you are all they hear about in this home and that they can no more doubt your existence and love for them than they can doubt ours as parents. I pray that you will be real to them all their days. Let me live a life they cannot ignore and feel compelled to imitate. Let them see where I take my problems and who gives me peace. Let them want to serve you because they have seen you work miracles.

DAY 16
The Stench of Leftover Sin

Traveling with children has never been a good experience for me, and I don't just mean the normal difficulties of traveling with small children, I mean it has proved excruciating. Now with airport security, it has become increasingly harder to travel with Brian and Kate. It is one thing to have to totally strip yourself to go through security, but entirely another to have to do so with two additional people, while keeping in mind the need to move quickly, as the people behind you sigh loudly. I don't know if you have noticed, but airports are not known for bringing out patience and longsuffering in people. Those challenges are enough; however, my daughter is not content with these challenges alone. Literally, since her birth, she has been trying to leave her mark on every airport or plane we enter. Traveling with my daughter has always proved to be nothing if not… fragrant. Four out of five airplane trips with my daughter have resulted in some of the most disgusting and smelly memories I have. Kate has repeatedly gotten a virus that doesn't rear its ugly head until we are on the plane, actually it did start once in the car on the way to the plane. But whatever the reason every time we get on a plane, we can be sure Kate will throw up. On our last trip, I actually packed changes of clothing for my husband and me as well as Kate. I was not disappointed. That child threw up all over both of us, one stewardess, and I think a little on a passerby. To say that the plane will never be the same would hardly cover the damage we did. Everyone was excited to see us go. After finally exiting the plane, a friend had come to retrieve us at the airport...*in their car*!!! With a quick prayer that God would keep us puke free in this car and car seat that did not belong to us, we were off. Kate managed to make it the whole way home without incident by the grace of God. I know it was by the grace of God because no sooner had I pulled her out of the borrowed car seat than she hurled all over me in the driveway. (I really should have put a disclaimer at the beginning of this one for those with weak stomachs!) At this point, I just got right in the bathtub with my daughter. We scrubbed up, and she went to bed while we proceeded to gather our things and unpack. For the next several hours, I kept smelling puke. It was lingering behind me like someone following me from a distance. I kept thinking it was my imagination, but it truly kept wafting over my shoulder. Finally I finished unloading our suitcases, collapsed in a chair, and ran a hand through my hair. It felt crunchy! I had caked on puke in my hair the whole time! I was too busy rushing around to take the time to even notice. That explained the occasional wafting fragrance.

This whole story reminds me of this guy named Simon. His story appears in Acts 8 and is a good read. He was this magician with a large following. People followed him because he amazed them. When Phillip came preaching about Jesus, many believed and were baptized, including Simon. Peter and John came to pray that the new believers would receive the Holy Spirit. When Simon saw this, he offered them money to show him how to do this great thing. Peter rebuked him saying, "Repent of this wickedness and pray to the Lord. Perhaps he will forgive you for having such a thought in your heart. For I see that you are full of bitterness and captive to sin" (Vs. 22&23). Simon immediately requested that they pray for him.

Talk about your not mincing words. Peter cut to the chase and spared no feelings in calling out Simon's return to habitual sin. Simon had made a living of exploiting magical acts for a long time. Old habits die hard. What is important here is that when confronted with the sin, Simon wasted no time in dealing with it. He did not try to excuse his behavior or rationalize it away. He just dealt with it. He began his Christian walk by getting rid of the lingering stench of sin that was still with him.

In parallel, I get this lingering smell and explain it away or make excuses instead of identifying the cause and taking it to Jesus immediately, who gently washes it away. If we leave any part of ourselves out of the cleansing process, we taint the fragrance of God to the world. We are the fragrance of Christ. We cannot afford to excuse our sin. Like Simon, we carry part of our old life and habits with us. They can be comforting and difficult to let go, even when the stench of them is too much to bear. It can be hard to admit that you are wrong. I myself have never dealt with this because I am never wrong, but I hear it can be quite painful. Somewhere my husband just went, "HA!" The Psalmist says, "For in his own eyes he flatters himself too much to detect or hate his sin" (Psalm 36:2). Beth Moore once said, "You see once we know how, we do not hesitate from rebuking Satan, because we despise him. On the other hand, we dearly love our own flesh. We have far more difficulty rebuking it." It is hard to take a rebuke and even harder to ask for one. But we are wise to do so. We are wise when we ask God to show us our sins that are hidden from our eyes. "Who can discern his own errors? Declare me innocent from hidden faults. Keep back your servant also from presumptuous sins; let them not have dominion over me. Then I shall be blameless and innocent of great transgression" (Psalm 19:12&13).

This brings me to my second point. God sometimes chooses a brother or sister in Christ to lovingly point out our sins to us. The problem with this is that as a whole, we in the body of Christ have become a bunch of wimps! There are no Peters or Pauls. We are instructed again and again in the Bible to bear with one another in our burdens, but somehow we take that as license to void all responsibility for others walks with Christ. If you smell the stench of sin on a brother or sister of Christ, you are responsible to them. We are ONE body.

We function best as a whole. There is a time to bear with one another in the growth process, but there is also a time for rebuking. The key to this is in Christ. We must ask Him for direction in each situation. If you are not walking closely enough with Christ to ask Him, then you are not called to do the rebuking, best take care of your own relationship. As you walk with Christ, He will make it clear to you who you are to bear with as they mature and those you are called to lead to repentance. They key is in relationship. Your motivation must be love. "We who are strong have an obligation to bear with the failings of the weak, and not to please ourselves. Let each of us please his neighbor for his good, to build him up" (Romans 15:1). Let me be clear when I say this should not be done in impatience or with self-serving desires. It is only to be done in obedience to Christ. It is for our "mutual up-building" (Romans 19).

We are called to be the fragrance of Christ. Our service and thanks are to be a sweet fragrance to Him. I don't want any lingering aroma of sin left. I want the stench completely gone. I want the world to be attracted to Christ with my life and not to be repelled by the fragrance of sin and death.

> "Wash away all my iniquity
> And cleanse me from my sin.
> For I know my transgressions
> and my sin is always before me.
> Cleanse me with hyssop and I will be clean;
> wash me and I will be whiter than snow.
> Create in me a pure heart, O God
> and renew a steadfast spirit within me.
> Do not cast me from your presence
> or take your Holy Spirit from me.
> Restore to me the joy of your salvation a
> and grant me a willing spirit, to sustain me."
> Psalm 51

Father, I pray that you will take off my blinders that keep me looking only in one direction. Help me to look back at what I have been and identify sin that needs dealt with. Help me to detect it because your Spirit is at work within me. Help me to see clearly when I am "full of bitterness and captive to sin." I pray with David in Psalm 17 that you would probe my heart and examine me at night that I may be able to say my steps have held to your path and my feet have not slipped. Give me the courage to love one other enough to be more concerned about the eternal than the temporal. Help me not to take any steps without your instruction, but to walk in obedience to your leading. Thank you that you are faithful to see if there is any offensive way in me and lead me in the way everlasting (Psalm 139:24).

DAY 17
None of My Business

The other day, Brian was screaming bloody murder because his sister would not share her Rapunzel Barbie. Finally when Kate could take it no more, she gave him the doll. He looked at it, gave it back and said, "No, I don't want it." He never wanted the doll; he only wanted what she had. My son has a room full of toys, but all he wanted was the one his sister had. If one of my children gets an additional crumb of cookie beyond the other, there is no end to the weeping and gnashing of teeth. Equality must never fail at dinner time either. "How many more bites do I need? Well how many does Brian need? But he didn't have as much as me." The comparisons are endless!!! "He got out of the tub first last night. I didn't get two stories!!" At this point I try to explain why the Constitution is wrong and we are not all equal. As a disclaimer, I am not recommending this tactic. This logic is totally lost on small children. Where is it that we learn to want what others have? Where do we get the idea that what we have is not enough, but whatever someone else has just might be enough?

This appeal for equality doesn't stop with children. I would love to say that it is an immaturity that we grow out of, but that wouldn't be true. For me it goes like this, "Why is she so pretty, why don't I have their house, why didn't God make me able to sing like her, why can't I have his car, why does she get to go there, how come they got away with that"…the comparisons are endless!

It is a comfort to me that Jesus knew our bent for comparison. He addressed it in Peter, His *rock*. Jesus had been instructing Peter that if he loved Him, Peter would feed His sheep. He also let Peter in on the future, painting a picture of Peter's death that was less than inspiring. As soon as Peter learned his future, he wanted to compare it to John's. "Peter turned and saw the disciple whom Jesus loved following them [to refresh your memory the "disciple that Jesus loved" was John]…When Peter saw him he said to Jesus, 'Lord, what about this man?' Jesus said to him, 'If it is my will that he remain until I come, what is that to you? You follow me!" (John 21:20-22). In Peter's eyes, his future didn't measure up with John's. It didn't seem fair and may have seemed to Peter that Jesus loved John more. My flesh responds with Peter that it doesn't seem fair. The key is that it didn't measure up in Peter's eyes, but Peter had limited vision and Jesus did not.

In the book of Matthew, there is a parable about laborers in a vineyard. The owner of the vineyard hired workers all throughout the day. When he found someone unemployed, he hired them. He did this up until the last hour of the workday. At the end of the day, all the laborers were paid the same wage. It was not dependent on the amount of work they accomplished or when they started. The laborers working the longest were very upset and took their complaints to the owner of the vineyard. This is what he said to those who did not receive what they perceived as equal wages, "Am I not allowed to do what I choose with what belongs to me? Or do you begrudge my generosity?"(Matt 20:15). We look on God's kindness as something He owes us, and it isn't. We begrudge His generosity when we are not thankful. God's kindness is meant to lead us to repentance (Romans 2:4). It is a gift, not something we are owed. We have done nothing for God; He has done all for us. The problem is our perspective. We look too long on what our neighbor has and neglect to see what we have received. We miss all our blessings because our eyes are fixed on the metaphorical Rapunzel Barbie our sister has.

If we could remember what we have in Jesus, the comparisons could cease. If we allowed what we know to be true, that we are dearly loved and that we are eternally secure, then what we have been given on earth would only have meaning in what it accomplishes for eternity.

"Let your eyes look directly forward, and your gaze be straight before you" (Proverbs 4:25). We are to fix our eyes on Jesus, not on our portion and not on our neighbors. If we fix our eyes on Him, we forget about equality. We realize that what we really want is forgiveness and complete love, and that is freely offered. If Jesus is what we gaze on, our circumstances fade to peripheral. They neither affect my view of today or my hope for tomorrow.

"So, what a blessing when God steps in and corrects you!
Mind you, don't despise the discipline of Almighty God!
True He wounds, but He also dresses the wound;
the same hand that hurts you, heals you."
Job 5:17&18 Message

O God, direct my gaze to you. Let me have holy tunnel vision. Distraction is one of the best tools Satan can use because it is subtle. Help me to recognize when I am gazing too long at a distraction. Help me refocus quickly, and if I don't, then do what you need to bring me back. Help me to practice thankfulness for the things that I am given so that they remain in focus as gifts from you. Help me train my eyes to see them for what they are, blessings that I don't deserve. Give me joy in the success of my friends and even strangers. Help me not to envy their blessings, but to rejoice with them.

DAY 18
These Boots Weren't Made For Walking

Boots. I have these great boots. They are cowboy boots that my husband got me for Christmas. I wear them a lot. They make a great swishy cowgirl noise when I walk and are totally in fashion. But, in the bathroom, nobody appreciates good boots, and the bathroom is where we had been for fifteen minutes when I decided that I may as well just kick off my boots and get comfy. You see, Brian had decided, just as we were leaving, that he needed to go potty. You should understand that, for Brian, a trip to the potty is an event. Hurrying him gets you nowhere. He has no sense of urgency or even awareness of time. As he sat on the toilet, he began to tell me a story. He was two at the time and two-year old stories are nothing if not detailed. There we sat. Instead of rushing, or worrying about how late we were going to be, I chose to resign myself to where I was and get some quality time with my son. It was a great decision. Brian told a wonderful story which involved him falling in the potty and being flushed down and down until Mommy saved him. Apparently I fished him out with the toilet brush. He even gestured for the story, flailing his arms so high twice that he almost *did* fall in the potty. I could have missed or rushed through this precious moment, but didn't. I am glad because his chubby little fingers and giggles are etched in my mind from that day as something I will remember when he is graduating from high school (wish I had pictures).

So much is missed in our daily schedules. So many moments, just like this one, that pass us by because they weren't penciled into our agenda, and we were rushing on to the next big event. I have a serious nostalgia for the days gone by when sitting on porch swings and watching the stars come out was an evening activity. Call me old-fashioned but there is something to that way of life. Nowadays we hurry, hurry, hurry. We are enticed to spend our time quickly before it's gone. Doesn't matter what you spend time on, but make sure you are spending, spending, spending. Don't stop, never slow down, use all those moments you have. Steal some from sleep if you can. Because we all know that time is something you can't get back! Feel the stress rising just after reading those sentences? "We are merely moving shadows and all our busyness ends in nothing" (Psalm 39:6). Nothing, our busyness ends in nothing. That means that nothing good comes of busyness. When you find yourself rushing to the next thing, stop and take off those boots. Because hurrying never accomplishes anything but tension. When I hurry, I forget things, loose my temper faster, take on a voice that doesn't sound human anymore, and often hurt someone I love. I have never gained a single thing by hurrying, I have only lost.

Moses says that there is a remedy for this; "Teach us to number our days that we may gain a heart of wisdom" (Psalm 90:12). So we have to number our days. Don't worry, this doesn't mean you have to figure out exactly how long you have left. Numbering your days involves noting the day as it passes. To do this, you stay planted in today. You get confused on the number if you spend time in too many yesterdays, or if you try to reach too far into tomorrow. You can only number your days as they happen. And Moses says that when we do, we gain a heart of wisdom. Wisdom is provided for the day you are in, when you need it. Wisdom applied to yesterday, doesn't change yesterday. Wisdom applied to tomorrow may or may not apply; we aren't there yet. The trick is paying attention to now. That is the only way not to waste time.

So how, how do we slow tomorrow without looking too far behind us? We pay attention to God. All time spent on Him enters into eternity. This doesn't mean you have to spend all day sitting at his feet. That would hardly be practical or possible. It means that He is your center. He is what pulls you, not the world. He can direct you to what is important and only He knows what will be important tomorrow. He gives the wisdom to know what you must cut out and what you must slow down for. He gives each of your moments. When you recognize that, it makes them all more precious. He took the time to plan all of your days and assigned each a number. Don't miss them by hurrying through them to the next. When you hear the voice of hurry in your head, recognize it as Satan's ploy to steal your moments. Stop and thank God for the time you are given and slow the clock by being all there. "Wherever you are be all there" advises Elizabeth Elliot. This sounds simple when there is really a lot to it. It is a practiced way of life. To start, thank God for the moment you are in, see what is really important in it. Practice making decisions to do fewer dishes and tickle your kids more. Be aware and attentive when your spouse is talking to you. Ask God to teach you to value what is really valuable.

God is timeless. The more you recognize Him in your moments, the more you see them as a gift and a blessing, and then they become timeless. Recognizing Him in each moment gives them value. It is done on purpose not on accident. You don't miss things that should be savored if you are giving each moment attention. Less time is lost and purpose is gained. So, take your boots off and stay awhile.

"Teach us to number our days that we may gain a heart of wisdom."
Psalm 90:12

Father, help me to slow time by recognizing your presence in my moments. Teach me to number my days in a healthy way, realizing that my time is short but valuable. Let me make decisions based on what you say is important and not what the world shouts to me. Show me how to deliberately recognize you and your plan for all my moments. Let me communicate to people that they are worth my time. Let me lavishly spend time with you by inviting you into every moment I have with a recognition of who you are and thanksgiving for the gifts you give.

DAY 19
Reflections of Glory

There is something so genuine about a baby's first glance in the mirror. When they understand all at once that they have a face, and it's staring back at them. "It's me! That's me!", they seem to shout without words. They are enchanted by who they are. Before the world tells them who they should be, before someone says their eyes are squinty or ears are too big, they are just enchanted by who God made them. Brian was looking in the mirror one day, I spoke and startled him out of his enchantment with himself. When I did, he caught my reflection in the mirror; his grin became huge. "It's Mommy! She is here too!", and then he began to wave his arms in the air and gut laugh as only he can.

"Anyone who listens to the word but does not do what it says is like a man, who looks at his face in the mirror and, after looking at himself, goes away and immediately forgets what he looks like" (James 1:23&24). I have always found myself compelled by this scripture. I want to know what I really look like. Not what my face looks like or if I am having a good hair day, but what I look like to God. When God shows me something that I didn't see in myself, it is usually something that needs to go. Once I have seen what God is trying to reveal to me, I really don't want to forget it. It's funny to think about forgetting what you look like, but it is actually easy to forget your faults because we don't want to think about them. I want to be haunted by the image God presents to me until He helps me change that image. "But the man who looks intently into the perfect law that gives freedom, and continues to do this, not forgetting what he has heard, but doing it will be blessed in what he does" (v.25). The answer lies in verse twenty-five. The man who looks not at himself in the mirror, but at the perfect law that gives freedom will be blessed. We are all so tempted to look at ourselves, to focus on ourselves, and to see only ourselves. We can even do this when we see errors in our life. We fixate on the error we see instead of looking into Jesus. He is what we should see because He is the perfect law James talks about. The law of the old testament didn't work. He came to perfect it, and in doing so, He replaced it (Hebrews 5). Looking into Jesus' eyes takes the pain out of our failure. It gives us the strength we need to take God's gentle discipline and let it sanctify us. Because we are counted as sons, we are disciplined because God disciplines those He loves. In Revelation, God tells us "Those whom I love I rebuke and discipline. So be earnest, and repent" (2:19). Of all the things I want to be, earnest is at the top of my list. I want to be earnest! I want my time to count. I don't want time to just pass; I want my time to mean something. If I don't live earnestly, then time *will* just pass. I want my pain on this earth to be getting me closer and closer to the glory that Jesus wants to reveal in me. Everyone will have pain, but I want to choose to let my pain count for something. I want to let it teach me the lessons God intends. If I can just see past my own reflection to that of Jesus then all else can fade.

I love how the Message states these verses, "But whoever catches a glimpse of the revealed counsel of God –the free life! - even out of the corner of his eye, and sticks with it, is no distracted scatterbrain but a man or woman of action. That person will find delight and affirmation in the action" (James 1:25). I want this scripture imbedded in my heart so that when I look in the mirror, I see more than the start of wrinkles and bags from sleepless nights. I want to catch another reflection. I want to say, "It's me!" and then, "It's Jesus!" I want to be able to see clearly past who I am, so that I can reflect who Jesus is. I want to recognize Him when I see reflections of Him covering me. Then when I go away and return, I don't want to see the same woman I left. My prayer is that we desire more reflections of Jesus because each glimpse we get of Him makes us want to see more. We can stick with it, because we are beloved daughters of God, and He disciplines those He loves so that we can take our place as sons. He has a plan and call on each of our lives; we just have to see past our own plans for ourselves to get it (Romans 11:29).

"Now we see but a poor reflection as in a mirror;
then we shall see face to face.
Now I know in part;
then I shall know fully, even as I am fully known."
1 Corinthians 13:12

"The people I love, I call to account-prod and correct
and guide so that they'll live at their best.
Up on your feet, then! About face! Run after God!"
Revelation 3:19 Message

Thank you that, according to Romans, you place a specific and irrevocable call on each of our lives. You choose to see what you made us to be. Thank you that when you look at me, it looks nothing like what I see when I look in the mirror. How I pray that you will see more of Jesus in me, and that I can see more of Jesus in me and recognize your work. Let me never look upon my reflection and mistake what I see for myself. Give me complete understanding that you are the only good found in me. Help me to heed the call of the Holy Spirit in my life and prompt me to swift obedience. Thank you for the grace you provide with your discipline and the fact that you love us enough to show us our errors and that because of that love; you cannot leave us in the pits where you find us.

DAY 20
Flutter No More

I have to share this story with you. It is not about my own child. God has blessed me with a dear friend who has a daughter the same age as mine. This story is about her child. Our children have been best friends from the womb. We actually have a picture of our pregnant bellies pressed together. Don't worry I won't share the photo!

Josie, my friend's daughter, was reading with her mother one night when they came upon a page that was not altogether right. Actually it simply wasn't all together. It was a beautiful pop-up book depicting a butterfly. This particular butterfly, however, seemed to have had some kind of altercation; its wings had been torn off. Mommy remembered this occasion and thought to use the book for a teaching moment. She questioned Josie, "Look what happened to the book. Do you remember tearing this?" Josie never missed a beat, pointed to the butterfly and clearly stated "Mimi" (Mimi is Josie's grandmother). At this point in the story, I could clearly picture Josie's face while accusing her grandmother of defacing her butterfly. I laughed so hard I lost my drink, mostly through my nose. The situation was not as funny to my friend at the time.

Once I became a little more composed, we discussed how disturbed we were by her daughter's ability to feign innocence at such an early age (she was only a little past the age of one). We did what any mother of a toddler at this stage does. We panicked and projected no small amount of heinous crimes into their futures, for which there would be no blaming Grandma. At our projected rate of decline, the girls would be joining Hell's Angels at the age of two. We have presently come to realize we may have overshot. The girls may not be as hopeless a case as we felt at the time.

What disturbed us the most was the fact that no one taught Josie to blame others. She picked it up all on her own. We all do. It is part of our innate sense of selfishness. "Let no one say when he is tempted, 'I am being tempted by God,' for God cannot be tempted with evil and he himself tempts no one. But each person is tempted when he is lured and enticed *by his own desire*" (James 1:13 & 14). It is as old as Adam in the garden, only he didn't have a Mimi to blame. He had an Eve. At the heart of Adam's accusation lies the real issue. He wasn't really blaming Eve; he was blaming God. If you will remember his exact words were, "the woman *you* gave me did this." He blamed God for the temptation. We do the same all the time. We stipulate that it is not our fault for choosing the wrong, but rather God's, for not giving us what we wanted to begin with. We think, "If only I had him as a husband, I wouldn't need an affair; If only God gave me their child, this wouldn't be happening; If I weren't so busy, I would have the energy to do things for God; If I were only blessed with money, it would fix all my problems." We blame God when we are not content.

Interestingly, God designed us to long for contentment, but we don't want to hear what it would involve to attain it. At our hearts core, we don't want the blame for our mistakes. It is much easier to shirk the responsibility on the nearest Mimi and play the victim, than admit that we aren't willing to do it God's way. "…There is no fear of God before his eyes. For in his own eyes he flatters himself too much to detect or hate his sin" (Psalm 36:1&2). It is important to remember that we are to blame, but there is One who willingly took our consequences. We didn't have to point the finger at Him. He willingly took our sins.

"Who can discern his errors?
Forgive my hidden faults.
Keep your servant also from willful sins;
may they not rule over me.
Then will I be blameless,
innocent of great transgression."
Psalm 19:12&13

"Keep steady my steps according to your promise;
and let no iniquity get dominion over me."
Psalm 119:133

"Search me O God and know my heart
Test me and know my thoughts
See if there is any offensive way in me
And lead me in the way everlasting."
Psalm 139:23&24

Father, make me quick to identify my faults. Do not let me be swept away by my own flattery. Give me a heart that cries, forgive my hidden faults and keep your servant from willful sins, may they not rule over me. Search me and know me that even my thoughts would please you.

DAY 21
<u>Walking Where I Can't See</u>

I had an epiphany this morning as I watched Kate walk by with a pillow and two blankets in tow. She and Brian had been playing in her closet. It was hilarious! The two of them got all hunkered down in there with the lanterns I got them for camping, and they sat turning their lanterns on and off and just giggled away. I was tempted to crawl in there with them, except with all the pillows and blankets they had, I wouldn't have fit. Anyway, Kate came past me with this huge load in front of her. She kept dropping things and stopping to try and pick them up. She had so much stuff piled up that she couldn't see where she was going so she ran into me and backed up to try again. I asked, "Baby do you need some help?" To which she replied, "Nope, Mommy, I got it." I then watched her walk ahead unable to see over the pillow covering here face until she ran smack into her door. After writing that, I realize that the question arises: Why didn't I stop her? It was really one of those things that you see happen in slow motion, and even though you see the expected outcome, there is nothing you can do about it. It wasn't that she didn't know the door was there; she had seen the door a million times. She was just carrying too much to anticipate its approach. Her stuff blocked her view.

Stuff ever blocked *your* view? Jesus says his yoke is easy (Matthew 11:30). He calls us to lay our burdens down and rest them with Him. That way they don't obstruct our view of Him. God is big enough to guide us through every part of life, even death. It's just that sometimes we carry our burdens in front of our face and then can't focus our eyes past them to Jesus. We cease to see Him guiding us, because we focus on the other stuff in front of our eyes. That is when Satan swoops in and shuts the door in front of us. It's not that I'm not aware of my own need. I just didn't see it coming, because I was focused where I shouldn't be while trying to do something I can't do alone.

Everyone carries different things in different seasons of life. Sometimes we are carrying too many things to see past them; sometimes our burdens aren't bad in themselves, but they weren't ours to carry. Sometimes we carry with us so much sadness that we are literally blinded by tears. During these times, we can't see our way in front of us because we focus on our grief. Maybe it's just the monotony of our daily tasks that add up and we can't see Jesus for sheer busyness. I have literally been behind a pile of dishes once that I really couldn't see past. It's usually at this point that we hit the door.

These are all signs that we should stop. I mean absolutely stop. Re-focus on Jesus before we find ourselves somewhere we never intended to be. It happens faster than we think. Sometimes we need to realize that God has it all under control. He doesn't actually need us. We may be wise to realize that putting down our load is what God intends us to do. If you find yourself under a load that is becoming an obstacle to seeing Jesus...put it down. I mean, do not pass go or collect two hundred dollars, PUT IT DOWN. There is nothing meant to get between Jesus and us. He may allow you to pick it back up, He may pick it up for you, or He may ask you to leave it where it lays. Once you get your eyes on Jesus, do what He asks. Don't rationalize or reason it away. DO IT. All of our effort and best intentions don't amount to a hill of beans. If Jesus isn't empowering us to do something, we are wasting our time, and that is something that we can't get back.

There is also another dynamic at work here. God will be a lamp to our feet and light to our path, but He isn't giving us a road map. Sometimes I run into the proverbial door because I didn't want to wait for God's light, and I tried to run ahead without Him. Try following God when He is behind you. Andrew Murray says that we are to follow God in such a way that we are "neither lagging behind nor getting ahead of Him." Sometimes I have even had the best of intentions, but I was taking time into my hands and it doesn't belong there. God will direct you, but He isn't going to give you directions. He keeps a firm grip on the map, and He is not giving it up. I know; I asked. He does let me giggle all I want and play with the lantern sometimes.

"The unfolding of your word gives light;
it imparts understanding to the simple."
"Keep steady my steps according to your promise,
and let no iniquity get dominion over me."
Psalm 119:130&133

Father, give me discernment. Satan wants nothing more than to make me ineffective, and he will use whatever he can to block my view. Make me one of "those who have their powers of discernment trained by constant practice to distinguish good from evil" (Hebrews 5:14b). Show me what I need to lay down. Give me faith to leave it or pick it up again when you ask. Let me take up only the yoke you ask me to. That is the only load you intend for me to bear and you equip me with everything I need for it (Hebrews 13:21). When I can't see you, you promise that I will find you when I seek You with all my heart (Jeremiah 29:13).

DAY 22
Make a Mad Dash for God

There is a specific run a child has when they are frightened by something unexpected. It is anything but graceful and often involves at least one fall in their haste to get away. Still, they can amazingly turn on a dime to reach you as fast as they can and climb up your frame. What the run lacks in grace, it makes up for in singular purpose: REACH MOMMY! They have complete confidence that you can tackle the problem. There may be other people between you and them, but they do not stop or detour. Their gaze is fixed on one point. They know that they need Mommy and no one else will do. Their perspective gives them clarity. They know their size and their smallness gives them insight into what *is* big. They know their limitations and where to take them.

Just like it gives me joy to be the refuge for my children, God wants to be the one we seek to hold on to when trouble comes. He wants to be our first stop with no detours. As soon as we see a sign of trouble, He wants us to start looking for Him. Often our first thought is to go to friends to make us feel better. Sometimes we feel the need to go to others because they are perceived as closer and more tangible. Sometimes it is so practiced, that it doesn't occur to us that we didn't pray about it first. Sometimes it seems I may go to them for a second opinion just to make sure God is right this time. But what I find most disturbing is that often, I go to them *first*.

I wish I didn't long for that human advice and feel the need to tell friends my problems when I know God wants to hear them. He never tires of hearing them. I never have to repeat myself or worry that he isn't paying attention. I don't have to wait for the morning or a convenient time. I don't have to be somewhere quiet or private. Anytime, anyplace is convenient for God.

I long to make a bee line straight for God and not stop for help from anyone else first. I want that fixed gaze that refuses to be distracted. Where did I get this idea that God doesn't have time or that He doesn't want to know all the details of my problems? It isn't from scripture. "The Lord longs to be gracious to you; He rises to show you compassion. For the Lord is a God of justice. Blessed are all who wait on Him" (Isaiah 30:18).

The pieces of my life, like a puzzle, are frustrating and don't always seem to fit together. They don't make sense unless I lay them out in front of God and he turns them just the right way so I can see how they fit. He is the only one who knows how they all go together. So when I turn to my friends, no matter how much they love me, we all just sit there and stare at puzzle pieces that we can't figure out. Human advice, no matter how thought through, is flawed. This doesn't mean you should never get a trusted friends opinion. It means that you should make sure the majority of time talking about the problem is spent with God. "I will instruct you and teach you in the way you should go; I will counsel you and watch over you" (Psalm 32:8). When I keep my dilemmas between me and God I find that it causes me less worry. I can wait in peace for the answer when I don't keep drudging up the details and repeating how terrible it all seems. It is so important, in lots of circumstances, to enlist the prayers of a trusted friend, but maybe not four or ten or however many you may be tempted to share with. There is only One who can actually fix the problem. Our time is much better spent discussing it with Him. Just like children, when we see our limitations, we need to remember where to take them.

"Cursed is the one who trusts in man, who depends on flesh for his strength and whose heart turns away from the Lord" (Jeremiah 17:5). In contrast, he states, "But blessed is the man who trusts in the Lord, whose confidence is in him. He will be like a tree planted by the water that sends out its roots by the stream. It does not fear when heat comes; its leaves are always green. It has no worries in a year of drought and never fails to bear fruit" (v.7-8).

"Cursed is the one who trusts in man, who depends on flesh for his strength and whose heart turns away from the Lord."
Jeremiah 17:5

Father, answer me when I call to you. Give me relief from my distress; be merciful to me and hear my prayer. Remind me that the Lord has set apart the godly for himself; the Lord will hear when I call to him (Psalm 4:1 &3). Make me like a tree that bears fruit in every season because I depend on you for my life giving water. Make my confidence be in you alone, so that I need have no fear. You are always near.

DAY 23
Snuggle Me

As a parent, one of the greatest joys in life is snuggling my children during the night. I was so tired one night at 2 a.m. when my son, Brian, woke up screaming. When I say screaming, you have no idea what I mean unless you know my son Brian. We call him the pterodactyl because of the sound that comes out of him when truly upset (yes that is how you spell the dinosaur, I know because I had to look it up). There is no warning, and it does not qualify as a cry. It is ear piercing and momentarily paralyzing. I struggled out of bed and into his room. When I say struggled I mean, found my glasses, robe, tripped on the dog, and hit my head on the bedpost. After making it through the dark living room, a challenge in and of itself, I found him standing with his blanket over his head waiting for me. He looked up at me with bleary eyes and breathed a sigh of relief as we snuggled up all comfy and warm while I reflected on how much I loved my little man. He looked so big, and it reminded me it wouldn't be long before this time of snuggling would be over. He will need me less and less. I remember thinking to myself that I wished someone was big enough to hold me. I would like to rest my head while someone listened to *me* breath evenly. I want a blanket to curl up with, in a soft lap, that smells good and safe. When the day has been long and the tasks unending, I want to rest in someone's lap.

I forget that my God *is* that big! I have a God who is larger than life. Why doesn't it occur to me that I can curl up in God's lap and rest? No really, I know the phrase sounds churchy, but God is our Abba. What Father doesn't enjoy his child like I enjoy mine? Jesus enjoyed children, and I imagine they flocked to him and wanted to be picked up into His arms. "Let the little children come to me…and He took the children in His arms, put His hands on them and blessed them" (Luke 10:14&16). "He will tend his flock like a shepherd; He will gather the lambs in his arms; He will carry them in His bosom, and gently lead those that are with young" (Isaiah 40:11). If He has arms willing to carry me, then I can definitely crawl up in His lap. I wonder what God would smell like if we were curled up next to Him. Maybe apple pie, the air after a thunderstorm, fresh brewed coffee, and peppermint sticks all rolled into one. That actually sounds horrible, so probably not all of those together but you get the point.

The idea that God is that accessible is sometimes lost on me. I know it to be true, but I can't get it into my heart. "How often I have longed to gather your children together as a hen gathers her chicks under her wings, but you were not willing!" (Luke 13:34). Jesus was looking down on the city of Jerusalem when He said this. They were His chosen children, and in their search for the Messiah, they totally missed Him. Jesus was too small for the picture they had painted. I don't want that to be true of me. In my search, I don't want to totally miss who God is because I believe what others or religions say about Him. We all have preconceived ideas about God that just aren't true. We don't even know where some of them came from. Sometimes I'm sure we think it is because we have no love here on earth that compares. We can't quite grasp Jesus. He loves us. That's just it! It does not depend on us at all! If we are rotten, He loves us. If we are good, He loves us. I still can't get my mind around that some days.

My favorite gospel was written by John. There is just something about him. He seems to me to have understood Jesus better than the others. Maybe it's because he was quieter than Peter. Maybe he listened and took more in. As moms we tend to be more like Peter, but I wish to grasp what John seemed to understand. He called himself the disciple that Jesus loved. He did it multiple times in scripture. I would never call myself that in public, much less write it down. Talk about ego! Except that it doesn't fit with the rest of John's personality, so it can't be ego. He just understood. He knew that he was loved of Jesus, specific to just him. It can be like that with us because Jesus specifically knows you, like no other. He is personal like that. Sometimes we take that away. We make him fit into how we understand fragile, priceless things. Like He is something marvelous that is just to be looked at and admired, but not touched.

"He will tend his flock like a shepherd; He will gather the lambs in His arms; He will carry them in his bosom, and gently lead those that are with young" Isaiah 40:11. Shepherds were touched; they got down and dirty with their sheep. They slept were the sheep slept; they ate where the sheep ate; they went where the sheep went. That is the marvel of God. He owns the cattle on a thousand hills; He has unlimited resources, the stars are at His fingertips, and He chooses to be with us. Why I will never understand, but I am beginning to believe it.

When we close our days and we are tired, we want to rest on God's lap and remind ourselves of His promises. If we can just meditate on how much we are the disciple that Jesus loves, we will sleep more soundly and securely. Sometimes we need a reminder of whose hands we are in. You can forget what you are surrounded by and take it for granted. When we dwell on the fact that God is holding us in His hands, it makes all our fears and cares seem so futile. They are an effort in uselessness. There is not a moment of our time on earth that God does not hold. So, we will curl up in His lap, where we can almost smell Him, and rest.

"I lift up my eyes to the hills;
From where does my help come?

My help comes from the Lord,
Who made heaven and earth?
He will not let your foot be moved;
He who keeps you will not slumber.
Behold, He who keeps Israel
will neither slumber nor sleep.
The Lord is your keeper;
the Lord is your shade on your right hand.
The sun shall not strike you by day,
nor the moon by night.
The Lord will keep you from all evil;
He will keep your life.
The Lord will keep
your going out and your coming in
from this time forth and forevermore."
Psalm 121

O God and Father make yourself real to me. I pray for an awareness of your spirit and its close proximity to me at all times. Let that awareness, increase my prayers; let me pray as one who talks with a friend on and off through the day. Thank you that yours is the only relationship I have that is never limited by distance. You charge no roaming fees. There is no one that I must compete for your attention with and you do not tire of me. Help me to learn to rest in your love for my need of approval. Forgive me for the times that I forget how big you are.

DAY 24
Let's Make a Deal

I am one of those great mothers who have read all the articles that say you should not give your child a crutch for sleep. However, I feel no obligation to apply it to my life. Both of my children sleep with a blanket and a paci. I figure if we are going to do something taboo, we may as well go all the way and have both. I am embarrassed to say that I even have a back-up blankie. That way when one is in the wash, we are still safe. Heaven forbid one should ever get lost!

Now that you know all about what not to do in parenting, let me give you a picture as to why. My son usually sleeps with his blanket and paci, but leaves them in the crib during his waking hours. However, lately he wants to play let's make a deal. He wants to take both with him when he gets up. We are working on this new development. I do mean working; it is a lot of work to keep both in the crib and get him out! He shows more ingenuity than his sister does and can move the crib bumper and drag out his blanket. Right now we are allowing him the blanket at least as a way of bargaining away the paci. He drags that stupid blanket everywhere. We just call him Linus and go on with our lives.

So recently I was thinking about Lot. I know you don't hear that a lot (Ha ha). Anyway I was, and it occurred to me how much I can be just like him. God decided to spare him from certain destruction, he and all his family. They just had to follow the angel's instructions and run to the hills. "When he [Lot] hesitated, the men [who were angels sent to save him] grasped his hand, and the hands of his wife and of his two daughters and led them safely out of the city, for the Lord was merciful on him. Flee for your lives! Don't look back, and don't stop anywhere in the plain. Flee to the mountains or you will be swept away" (Genesis 19:16&17). They were instructed not to look back, probably because God knows how hard it is to give up what you know. His wife did not obey and was turned to a pillar of stone. Now it's easy to say that she should have just been thankful to be alive, but I understand her temptation. I can't count the times I have "looked back" and God has been merciful. The angels urged Lot and his daughters to the hills, but Lot couldn't resist; he begged them to have more mercy on him, and instead of fleeing to the mountains, he requested a small town nearby instead. God granted his request (v.20&21).

I never fail to be amazed at the mercy of God, and God willing, I never will. Even though God's plans were better, He allowed Lot his own way. God is so patient with man. "How much higher His ways than ours and His thoughts than our thoughts" (Isaiah 55:8&9). How many times in my life has God said alright, have it your way, you just don't understand. He doesn't force us, He tries to coerce, and He seeks to open our eyes, but He never forces. If I could see the times that God has let me have my own way and how much better his way was than mine, I feel sure I might be sick. We deal and whine and bargain for our own way, and then are surprised when we are not trusted with much. God cannot trust us until He knows we will do it His way. He can't trust us with His plans when we constantly try to make them our plans. "Many are the plans in a man's heart, but it is the Lord's purpose that prevails" (Psalm 19:21).

"I'll go God, but can I just take my blanket? I'll go God, but can I just take my…girlfriend, family, new car, children, bank account, or favorite outfit? I will go, but I just need my Pastor, accountability partner, or best friend. I can't do it without…because I need that comfort." It's like those people who ask to be buried with their baseball cards. This never actually made sense to me. When I go, I don't want to be buried with Pete Rose, maybe a cheesecake, but not Pete Rose. They don't see that where they are going there will be no use for these things. What we don't see is that if we can't go with just God, He can get no use from us.

I was thinking about Brian's blanket and how much it can annoy me. Then I realized that one day that crazy blanket will be so precious to me. I am sure by then he won't be dragging it around and will hardly remember it, but it will be precious to me. How much more does God treasure the things that we give Him? The things we freely give back to Him in obedience. They are His keepsakes and treasures forever in a place that moth and rust can never destroy (Matthew 6:20).

"Many are the plans in a man's heart,
but it is the Lord's purpose that prevails."
Psalm 19:21

O God, make me increasingly less attached to the things I call mine. So that when I am called home, there is nothing that pulls me to look back. Help me to trade what I cannot gain for what I can never loose. Give me an outpouring of your Spirit to replace any void. Thank you that only you can make me content.

DAY 25
<u>Startle</u>

One of my favorite things about infants is the startle reflex. My son Brian's was the best. At the slightest movement or noise he would shoot his hands to the sky as if someone had just yelled, "stick 'em up". It made me laugh every time. My daughter used to do this in church when the band would begin to play. She would be asleep and her little hands would shoot up to the sky. My husband would tell people, "She's just charismatic like her mother." Infants feel totally insecure in the world. They have spent nine months tucked away in the safety of their mother's womb. Even their own movements sometimes scare them. I am always tickled at how skittish they can be. I spend a lot of time wishing that they would get back some of that timidity. When they start to grow, they change from being scared of everything to scared of nothing!! This change can take years off of a mother's life. I remember an occasion that took several off of mine. Some friends had come over to help with the installation of our pool. While the wives stood by looking ravishing, the men were hard at work putting in the liner. When we checked to make sure they were doing it *the correct way* (since they were doing it without our help), we found a scene that struck terror in our hearts. My husband Pete was slinging Kate across the entire length of the pool in about an inch of water. (I should mention that Pete is her father otherwise I might have killed him). He, and one of our friends, slid her back and forth like they were bowling. She had complete faith that this was totally safe; she felt free to delight in the ride without hesitation. I, on the other hand, tried not to watch. One of my friends was already in the house looking up the number for Child Protection Services.

There are two things that Kate knew that I should have taken to heart. She knew her ride did not depend on her ability, and she knew that she could trust her Dad.

Kate knew that her ability didn't matter. When my children run and jump into my arms, it doesn't ever matter if they don't get a good hold on me because I have a hold of them. If I let go of them, they may hang on a moment, but they won't last. They will eventually fall. Sometimes I fear failure, not because I don't trust God, but because I am afraid that I will waiver. What I need to realize is that my strength doesn't matter. How long I hold on does not depend on me, but on Christ. "Not that I have already obtained all this, but I press on to take hold of that for which Christ Jesus took hold of me" (Philippians 3:12). *He* has taken hold of me; *He* will do the work in me. When God chose me for the task at hand, He knew I wasn't capable of it. Children are a precious example of this because they carry no guilt in being carried. They know when they aren't capable and have no doubts about who is able to help them. Once Jesus has taken hold of you, it is completely in His power to complete the work in you, and He is faithful to do it. It doesn't depend on your ability to hold Him; it depends on His ability to hold you.

Kate knew her father; experience taught her that she could trust that he would not hurt her. When God comes up with plans for me that seem no safer than getting slung across a pool, I panic. My startle reflex kicks in, and I begin to rationalize why this isn't a good or safe idea. Instead of looking into my Father's eyes when He says jump, I look down at the ground. I reason that it is too high or rationalize that there are better, safer ways to get down that will produce the same result. But that's just the point. I assume the desired result is to get me to the ground when really the ground has nothing to do with it. God's desired result is for us to jump and trust Him to get us to His desired location, be it the ground or His arms. His desired result is for us to trust Him to work out the details and destination. All He wants from us is a focused, sometimes determined, gaze into His eyes and not the ground. Then we can jump, knowing our destination matters less than the arms we find ourselves in. The key to trust is in knowing the arms. Getting to know them involves that we focus on how faithful they have been. When you choose to focus on God's provision in daily life, you expect it for the future. So start documenting how faithful God is to you. It will increase your faith.

A. W. Tozer says that, "Faith is the gaze of a soul upon a saving God". It takes a consistent gaze. It takes discipline and concentration, and it is a choice. Where will you choose to look?

"Let us hold fast the confession of our hope without wavering,
for He who promised is faithful."
Hebrews 10:23

"The one who calls you is faithful, and He will do it."
1 Thessalonians 5:24

Father, help me to see your eyes and not the ground. Let me focus less on the process and more on you. Teach me to remind myself of all of your provision from the past. Teach me to meditate on your promises. Teach me to hold my plans and my destination loosely. Keep me from rationalizing until I don't obey your call. Thank you for your heart and the safety that lies in you being Love. Not full of love, or with love, but Love itself. Thank you that perfect love casts out all fear (1 John 4:18). Remind me that you are faithful to complete the work that you start in me. Thank you that you do not depend on my faithfulness but on yours.

DAY 26
True Healing

"Jesus healed it Mommy!" These were the words of my three year old when she woke up from her nap. She had a small sore on her lip, and we had been putting medicine on it for days. Before nap, we prayed for Jesus to heal it; after nap, it was visibly better. When she assured me that Jesus healed her lip, I smiled and said, "I'm sure He did." I humored her while in my head thinking, "that Neosporin really does the trick." Looking at my daughter dancing around her room, I was struck with my disbelief. Just because it was small doesn't mean that Jesus didn't heal it. We had put medicine on it for a week; what made it work all of the sudden?

If you were to ask me if Jesus still does miracles I would answer a resounding yes. I believe He can and does heal cancer and prevent accidents in miraculous ways. So why didn't I believe He cared enough to heal Kate's lip? I am quick to attribute it to the medicine. In Kate's simple world Jesus is in charge of everything. We believe that too, but we complicate our world or rather our world becomes complicated. We simply stop seeing that Jesus is in charge of everything. We fancy ourselves as key players of our destinies, and sometimes even our children's. There are so many times a day when things are attributed to chance or normal causes when what has actually happened is that we have simply stopped seeing Him.

When I asked Kate about Jesus healing her lip, she said He came in her room while she was sleeping. How do I know He didn't? He is much more likely to heal her with her complete belief and trust in Him than me with my doubt and disbelief. So, I am choosing to believe that He healed her lip out of His love for her. I am also remembering that He loves me too and waits for me to ask for healing in so many places that I don't, because I don't believe He will. Oh I would say it out loud, but I wouldn't, in my heart, really expect healing.

My favorite verses in the book of Mark revolve around a parent and child. A father came to Jesus with a child who had been possessed by a spirit that inflicted harm on the child. The father was distraught; he had already taken his son to the disciples who couldn't help him, so he petitioned Jesus, "If you can do anything, have compassion on us and help us" (Mark 9:22). The *if* always gets me here. *If* Jesus can do anything. Jesus can do everything! Let me say that again because it sounds so trite that we forget how true it is. Jesus can do everything! He responds to the father, "If you can! All things are possible for one who believes. Immediately the father of the child cried out and said, 'I believe; help my unbelief'" (v. 23&24). After reading this, I have repeated it to God countless times. I do believe, and in the same breath I cry, help my unbelief. That is why I have less trouble believing that Kate's lip was healed by Jesus. She believes that Jesus can do everything. My prayer for her is that her faith will not dwindle as she becomes more mature by the world's standards. My prayer for us is that we can grow less "mature" by the world's standards and grow faith like a child.

Take another look in Mark with me, at a different situation and different outcome. "He could not do any miracles there, except lay his hands on a few sick people and heal them. And he was amazed at their lack of faith..." (Mark 6:5). This verse is talking about Jesus in His hometown. They refused to believe. Because of their refusal they saw less of God's glory. I don't want to refuse God because of my unbelief and therefore limit what He does with my life. I want to believe Him for great things.

Believe that God can work miraculously in your life, not just for physically healing but for spiritual rebirth and healing. Jesus can do *everything*!

"And without faith it is impossible to please Him,
for whoever would draw near to God must believe that He exists
and the He rewards those who diligently seek Him."
Hebrews 11:6

"Then Jesus said, 'Did I not tell you that if you believed,
you would see the glory of God?'"
John 11:40

I cry out with the man in Mark "I do believe, forgive my unbelief." Don't leave me here in my pitiful faith. I know that means you will stretch me. I confess that at times that scares me so much, but I want to be useful to you. If I don't have faith, I am not of much use. You have said in your word that without faith we cannot please you. God I want to please you. I want to draw near to you. Make me into something that pleases you.

DAY 27
Whistle While You Work

Kate can sing about anything. She will often just walk around singing everything she is doing or thinking. She will sing about playing with dolls, brushing her teeth, or walking down the stairs. Her songs always seem to incorporate "Jesus and God." In her mind the two must always be sung about together. She seems to have an early understanding of the trinity. It's beautiful and comical at the same time. It always leads me to think of the music of Heaven, because of her sincerity. She sings at the top of her lungs, though sometimes off key, but she sings just the same. Singing gives her joy. She does it to the point that Brian will start screaming, "Stop! Stop! Stop singing!" He is just as sincere in his hopes for a moment's peace as she is in her song. What is striking about Kate's song, although, is her ability to sing it over everything. She sings to Jesus, with all her own made up words and phrases, but to Jesus nonetheless. In this way, she is happy no matter what she is doing.

We are instructed to sing in scripture. However, this instruction is seldom taken to heart. We sing in church on Sunday morning before the sermon; that is one of my favorite parts (my husband likes to call it the pre-game). But if singing is worship, why aren't we doing it the rest of the week? Shouldn't we do it outside of church too? Understand that I am not saying that we should keep hymnals in the kitchen and all throughout the house. I am not suggesting that we spend our days in one organized chorus of song never ceasing. That only works out in musicals starring Nuns and Julie Andrews. However, if we are instructed to praise, then we shouldn't just do it on Sundays. I am also not suggesting that you add things to your to do list. I have a much simpler solution. Kate's song *is* the solution. She doesn't stop what she is doing for a quick song break; she sings over her action. And when she does, her joy is infectious. I need to learn to sing over my daily activities. How much different could that make the acts of brushing my teeth, folding the laundry, making dinner, or vacuuming (I know you just got a picture of me singing while brushing my teeth. Ha! Ha!). It doesn't have to be a real song, it doesn't have to be organized and it doesn't even have to be musical. It just has to express praise to God. When we praise God, we bring Him into the moment. The more moments we bring Him into, the more joy we experience because He is our joy.

Mother Theresa once wrote, "The work we do is only our love for Jesus in action. If we pray the work…if we do it to Jesus, if we do it for Jesus, if we do it with Jesus…that's what makes us content." All of the work I do is my love for Jesus in action, which does include changing poopy diapers, and cleaning toilets, ladies. I know it seems that those tasks can't be done for Jesus, but when I love others, Jesus says I am loving Him. "…Truly I say to you, as you did it to one of the least of these my brothers, you did it to me" (Matthew 25:40). When you feel that taking care of your family is unimportant in the spiritual realm, it is untrue. The work you do out of love for your family, with a right heart, is sacred to God.

When I do my work in a spirit of complaint, it becomes exhausting and at the end of the day I am spent and grumpy. When I do my work for people, even people I love, I am sometimes left feeling bitter and unrecognized. It is a rare 2 year old who thanks you for the daily tasks that keep their world afloat. In contrast, if I do my work unto Jesus, in service to Him; if I do it for Jesus because my love for

Him compels me to love others; if I praise him in song while I work then He is with me. All of these combined bring joy. If He is with me in the night when I am washing that last dish, knowing that in a few hours I start all over again, then I can do that act with joy because of His presence in my kitchen. His presence takes all loneliness out of menial jobs. His presence can make my home a cathedral. If I sing, even in my spirit, and recognize that my work is for Him, then it becomes meaningful and remembered. When I praise God and sing in my work, it becomes an offering to God. Then it stands for something, its worth is increased tremendously and the time is made holy instead of begrudged.

There is another aspect to praising while you work that I came across while reading a passage in 1 Corinthians about speaking in tongues. These verses made me contemplate how the act of joy in service blesses the receiver. They are not only blessed by your actions but by the spirit of God that you bring into the moment. It allows them to share in your praise. "Well then, what shall I do? I will pray in the spirit, and I will also pray in words I understand. I will sing in the spirit, and I will also sing in words I understand. For if you praise God only in the spirit, how can those who don't understand you praise God along with you? How can they join you in giving thanks when they don't understand what you are saying? You will be giving thanks very well, but it won't strengthen the people who hear you" (1 Corinthians 14:15-17). When you are giving thanks and praise to God while you work, it strengthens the people who hear you. And if they are not believers, it sheds light on the joy of Christ. How you work can speak volumes to them about the love you have received. Joy and song in everything you do speak to a world that has no hope. It speaks of a joy they might not yet understand in their spirit but can see with their eyes. Your children will also learn from your example how to work as an offering to God instead of grumbling and complaining. As a mother, I can tell you a little less whining and more whistling while we work can change the whole atmosphere of a day and make it sacred.

The next time you are doing the job you hate the most, try singing. Sing a song that gives praise and thanks to God, even under your breath, and it will change your work into an offering to God. It will also change your countenance, and if you are like me, anything that prevents a wrinkle or two is well worth the effort. It's like a free face-lift.

"Through Him [Jesus] let us continually offer up
a sacrifice of praise to God, that is,
the fruit of lips that acknowledge His name."
Hebrews 13:15

Father, teach me that I can make any moment holy by singing praise. Everything I do can be an act of worship if I chose to acknowledge you in the moment and think on my work as an offering. Make my daily domestic life an offering of praise and worship to you. Open my eyes to see Heavenly moments all around me. Let me teach my children that work has value only when it is done unto you. Teach me to pour love into my family as an offering to you, as you have poured love into me. Let the picking up of wet towels, scraping of plates, and washing of dishes daily be turned into something sacred.

DAY 28
Innocent

There is no time like bedtime. After the unending ploys for "one more drink" and "stay with me please", my children are the most loveable at bedtime. They are all clean and snuggly and they are full of love. One more kiss turns into seven more kisses and they know they are winning, but they are just so lovable at this hour. Finally their eyes close and they can't fight anymore (which is a considerable victory after what has seemed like a WWF event). They have run all day and when they actually fall asleep, they are totally calm and peaceful. A child sleeping is one of the most beautiful things in the whole world (and I don't mean because they are finally quiet). They are so untainted and innocent, completely peaceful. In truth, this is one of the only times my son appears innocent and not just ornery. This innocence that draws me to stand and watch them is the picture of our standing in Christ.

We, who are in Christ, are also called to be innocent. "For your obedience is known to all, so that I rejoice over you, but I want you to be wise as to what is good and innocent as to what is evil" (Romans 16:19). The word innocent has three important synonyms to consider: pure, harmless, and blameless.

We can be innocent to what is evil by remaining pure and uneducated to what is evil. This does not mean that we are unaware of its existence. It means that we do not allow evil a part in our thoughts or our actions. We purify our thoughts and actions. "How can a young man keep his way pure? By guarding it according to your word" (Psalm 119:9). You cannot taste of evil and remain pure. If you accommodate evil, that means you are excusing it in your life. There is no place for excusing evil on any level. We who follow Christ are instructed to, "Hate what is evil; cling to what is good" (Romans 12:9b). The message translates this verse, "Run for dear life from evil; hold on for dear life to good." You cannot run in two directions at once. You must either run in the direction of evil or run in the direction of good. "I will run in the way of your commands for you have set my heart free" (Psalm 119:32). It is a choice to run in the way that will set your heart free. The more we run in the right direction, the freer we are to experience the life God intends for us.

Webster's defines harmless as lacking capacity or intent to harm or injure. We aren't just to avoid evil; we are not to plan for it. It should not be our intent. We should lack the capacity for it. Capacity means the potential or suitability for holding, storing, or accommodating. Realize that intent can be the thoughts and intentions of the heart. Even thinking unkindly about others has harmful intent. We are not to be a vessel that accommodates any evil. We cannot let evil be at home in us. We are to be so unaccommodating, that evil doesn't even feel comfortable around us. So that we may "...be blameless and innocent, children of God without blemish in the midst of a crooked and twisted generation, among whom you shine as lights in the world" (Philippians 2:15). If we look just like the world in its knowledge of evil, then we do not shine as a light to them, because functionally we are just the same as they are. Our difference should make them a little uncomfortable. It points to their need for a Savior.

The third synonym for innocent is blameless. We are only blameless in Christ because He took our blame. What so many people miss is that Christ is able to keep you that way. "But test everything; hold fast what is good. Abstain from every form of evil. Now may the God of peace himself sanctify you completely, and may your whole spirit and soul and body be kept blameless at the coming age of Christ. He who calls you is faithful; He will surely do it." (1 Thessalonians 5:21-24). We are encouraged again that being kept blameless has everything to do with holding fast to what is good and abstaining from evil. God is faithful. He will keep us from evil. The work is done by Him, but I am responsible for being obedient; I must be wise to what is good and choose to remain innocent to evil. "Blessed are those whose way is blameless, who walk in the law of the Lord" (Psalm 119:1). We must choose to walk in the law of the Lord and remain blameless.

This is not something you can just will yourself to do. Paul tells us, "I know that nothing good dwells in me, that is, in my flesh. For I have the desire to do what is right, but not the ability to carry it out" (Romans 7:18). Without Jesus we don't have the ability to carry this out. But we, who have Jesus, have the means and responsibility to run for dear life from evil. When we spot it, we should immediately turn from it. Immediately! Don't let Satan get time to help you reason it away. When you recognize evil, turn and run for dear life to good. For some this may mean that you recite scripture and redirect your thoughts, for others it may mean that you must find a bible and immerse yourself in it for an hour. However it looks, whatever it takes, that is what you do. Jesus is waiting for you to ask for help. "Consequently, He is able to save to the uttermost those who draw near to God through him, since he always lives to make intercession for them" (Hebrews 7:25). He *always* lives to make intercession for us. He is *always* available. In Christ we can remain innocent, pure, harmless, and blameless. Without Christ we are incapable to be even one of them. With Christ, we can run for dear life to good, and then rest and sleep as innocent children.

"Hate what is evil; cling to what is good."
Romans 12:9b

Father, make me wise to what is good. Help me to clearly see the things I should be about on this earth. Make me equally aware of what is evil that I may flee it. Make my feet fast to run away from evil into the arms of Good. Thank you for Jesus and His promise to be with me always. I do not ever face evil alone. Thank you for the promise that you will not leave me as you found me. You are faithful to do the work in me. Make me swift to obey. Purify my thoughts and actions. Keep me blameless. Let me not plan harm or even entertain harm, but rather love. Thank you that in Christ I am innocent.

DAY 29
Monkeys in Your Pocket Book

I am blessed to be a mom with a vivid imagination, and it appears my daughter has that same imagination. It makes her easy to entertain, but oh the messes we clean up. However, it is definitely all worth it. She received a toy Noah's ark for Christmas this last year. It includes the boat and sets of two of every kind of animal that God ever made...ever. Those animals, or "aminals", as she calls them, have been everywhere. They travel two-by-two all over our house. They have been in purses, baskets, potty chairs, pockets, pillowcases, cabinets, sandboxes, and every toy they can fit in two-by-two. I kid you not, they are never alone. Rarely will you find a zebra in the dishwasher by itself; he is usually accompanied by his twin and at least another couple of giraffe's. I was recently amused to find that all of the animals had migrated two-by-two from the ark to the trunk of Kate's toy car. It has a small storage compartment she can open right under the seat. She was perched on top of all the animals driving them around the living room. She was very proud that they all fit, with their partners, and even though the lid would not close, felt a great sense of accomplishment. I couldn't help wondering if Noah was in heaven right then thanking God that even if the boat had been smelly after 40 days with all those animals, at least God's plan had not involved them traveling under the smelly diaper of a two year old. Sometimes all you need to be thankful is the reminder of the circumstances God *could* have used.

There is a point, and I promise to get there, but not quite yet. This story isn't over. These days I teach part-time. I am blessed with a job where I work few hours, my daughter goes with me, and all my high school students have the opportunity of knowing her. Some even get to participate in her care. They are all involved in our life, some days way too much. Today while getting ready to go out the door, my adorable 2 year old handed me my purse with a smile. She had been swinging it around while I was packing her lunch, cleaning up breakfast, and putting in the laundry. After arriving at school, one of my seniors asked what time it was. I reached for my cell phone to tell him and pulled out a monkey. Knowing my daughter as I do, I handed one monkey to my student and began to search for his friend. I found not only the partner in crime but also a bunch of bananas. My daughter thinks ahead. Apparently the monkeys needed a field-trip to change their scenery, and she wanted to make sure they weren't hungry.

Though this story is quite funny, my reason for telling it is rather serious; wherever you are, it is where God put you. Hear that again…wherever you are, it is where *God* put you. He intended it. He knows where you need to be effective; He knows your abilities; He knows your stamina; He knows you.

He will not call you to do anything that He doesn't equip you for. God will "…equip you with everything good that you may do his will" (Hebrews 13:21). You might think you are in a position where you have little affect on things, but if God put you there, He has a design for it. Maybe you aren't a monkey in a pocket book, but you feel like you're in the dark. You may be a stay at home mom, a teacher, grocery bagger, dental assistant, student, or nuclear physicist. It doesn't matter. God does not always have to put you somewhere glorious or high-profile to use you. Don't short change his plans. He provides some way for you to glorify him in every stage of your life. God tells us right in scripture how He equips us, "All Scripture is breathed out by God and profitable for teaching, for reproof, for correction, and for training in righteousness, that the man of God may be complete , equipped for every good work"(2 Timothy 3:16&17). Scripture is packed full of the nourishment we need, just like bananas. You can depend on it. God does not make mistakes in choosing you or in providing everything you need for good. "For God's gifts and his call are irrevocable" (Romans 11:29).

There are times God can't use me until something changes, and often in my life I need a change of scenery or rather perspective. I don't see things the way God does so He has to get my attention and help me see them differently. God has often used new circumstances to affect a change of my perspective. They may have been new seasons in life or huge moves to new states. In retrospect, I can say that God has never put me anywhere that He didn't mean to place me. His plans for you may not always be clear, but He knows where you are going and what you will need. He never for a moment forgets where you are, even if He puts you there for quite some time. No matter how long you have been where you are, God will sustain you. He always does, and you can depend on it. Sometimes the only way my perspective could be changed was a change of scenery. One of my trips ended up being a permanent move, and I can't tell you how it has instrumentally changed my whole life. (Mostly because I take rabbit trails and we would be here forever.)

"As the heavens are higher than the earth, so are my ways higher than your ways, and my thoughts than your thoughts" (Isaiah 55:9). Because God's ways are so perfect, He can facilitate a change in us that we could never affect for ourselves, but to make it happen He has to put us somewhere unfamiliar, or painful, or simply out of the way for awhile. He will never put you anywhere you aren't meant to go or to fit.

The next time you find yourself in a pocket book with a bunch of monkeys, wondering how in the world you got there; remind yourself that He has a plan even when it's dark. Remember that you are always safe because of where He is, not where you are. He might even send you a friend, who can hold the flashlight, so that you can go two-by-two through the dark and strengthen each other.

"As the heavens are higher than the earth,
so are my ways higher than your ways,
and my thoughts than your thoughts."
Isaiah 55:9

Father thank you that you never ask me to do anything you don't equip me to do. Help me as I seek to follow the path you lay out for me. I live in the dark, but thank you that you promised to be the light to my path. When I find myself somewhere I don't want to be, remind me to ask what your purpose may be. Remind me that you do have a purpose for every event in my life. Give me your thoughts on my circumstance and a new perspective.

DAY 30
<u>Fear</u>

Planes flew overhead and I ran for the door. I anticipated the reaction to the booming noise. My son, Brian, ran screaming into the house with eyes closed and chubby little hands pressed so hard on his ears it looked painful. He was running so fast that he plowed right into me, never opening his eyes, climbed right up me, and cried "Mommy make it stop!" It was truly pitiful.

My precious son has a very real fear. Any loud noise terrifies him to the point of shaking all over. This story will require a little background information. The reason he has no tolerance for loud noises, stems from the fact that our family home was destroyed by a tornado last year. There was literally no house left standing except the pantry we were in. In this pantry, we were kept safe under the hand of God. These words do not do the protection of God justice. If I were to tell you all of His provision through and after the tornado, time would fail me. However, for a two and a half year old it is hard to keep that perspective. Brian tends to panic when anything is loud. He covers his ears with his hands to try and make it stop. His reaction to scary things isn't that far from my own. But I have learned a secret. Instead of covering my ears and trying to make the sound go away, I focus my hearing on something until it becomes louder than the fear. You see my whole life people would tell me that bad things wouldn't really happen. Even as a child I saw flaws in that argument. I was not willing to bank my anxiety on the statistically small possibility that my fear wouldn't actually come to pass. I was told that I would never actually experience a tornado. I am here to tell you, that argument literally blew right out the window.

Fear is a real thing. The reason my poor son cannot drown out the entire sound that is scaring him is because it is real. No matter how hard he presses his little hands in on his ears, he knows that what is causing the sound is still there. It cannot be made to go away or ignored out of existence. It is a thing, therefore it is a noun. But fear can also be a verb. When fear governs our actions, it is a verb we are allowing to control us. As Christians we are called to keep it as a noun and not participate in its action. You see we can do two things with Fear: we can either see fear as the noun it is and take it to God who puts it behind Him and stands between us, or we can listen to fear and give it permission to act in us and become a verb. It will continue to manipulate our minds until it controls all of our actions.

The only thing that actually makes the fear go away is to replace it with something equally loud. Or I should rather say something much more powerful. The truth of God's word is all that can comfort a soul. This is how "perfect love casts out all fear." Jesus *is* perfect love and Jesus *is* the word made flesh (John 1:14). "There is no fear *in* love, but *perfect love* casts out fear. For fear has to do with punishment, and whoever fears has not been perfected in love" (1John 4:18). That perfect love that casts out all fear is a person. When we have a relationship with this person, He can cast out our fear. We cannot just simply follow a list of rules, live a "good" life and imagine nothing bad will happen to us. How one could entertain the health, wealth and prosperity gospel after reading scripture is beyond me, but the reality is that some people act according to a belief just like this. That somehow if God is on our side it means that nothing bad will ever happen to us and we will only experience prosperity. That isn't true. Our comfort is that *when* bad things happen perfect love, Jesus, will never leave us. He is with us even to the end of the age.

You fill your mind with what is absolutely true, not what might possibly become true. In C.S. Lewis's, *Screwtape Letters*, Lewis writes letters from the perspective of a demon to his nephew, training him how to do battle with Christians. This is the advice he presented to his nephew when addressing the subject of anxiety and fear, "Let him [the Christian] regard them [tribulations] as his crosses: let him forget that, since they are incompatible, they cannot all happen to him, and let him try to practice fortitude and patience in advance. For real resignation, in that same moment, to a dozen different and hypothetical fates, is almost impossible, and the Enemy [God] does not greatly assist those who are trying to attain it: resignation to present and actual suffering, even where that suffering consists of fear, is far easier, and is usually helped by this direct action." See, Satan knows that if he can distract us with preparation for all the hypothetical tragedies in the future, we are not focused on God. We are distracted from the present moment, the moment in which God promises help for our trouble. "So don't worry about tomorrow, for tomorrow will bring its own worries. Today's trouble is enough for today" (Matthew 6:34). God promises to be there in our future, but does not promise to give peace ahead of the need. Otherwise there would be no need to abide in Him moment by moment. When we are distracted by future worries, the now takes us off-guard and that is where Satan wants us, paying no attention to the now, and fearing for the future.

> "There is no fear *in* love, but *perfect love* casts out fear.
> For fear has to do with punishment,
> and whoever fears has not been perfected in love."
> 1John 4:18

God, remind me that perfect love is only found in you. Perfect love is your son. You offer yourself to me. Thank you that there is not one moment in all my days that you have not prepared. Remind me that the only preparation I need to make for my future is to trust you with it. I cannot guess what time will bring, but you hold time in your hand. All my days are but a breath (Psalm 39:5), and yet you love me still. Help me look only at what I am given one day at a time. Thank you that you supply me with all I need for that day, so I have nothing to fear.

DAY 31
<u>Invitation Only</u>

As Kate was going to bed one night, she got a funny look on her face. I knew the look. A question was coming. It was a huge one in her mind; you could actually watch the wheels turning. Now this could range from no-brainers like, why do we need to brush our teeth, to questions that really require thought such as, where do babies come from. Children have no inhibitions. Keep in mind this question was coming from my girl, Kate, a child who is not limited by social boundaries or vocabulary, so I prepared my brain for the worst.

She looked up at me with those angelic eyes and said, "Mommy, where is God?" I mentally weighed my options. I could respond with a simple "in Heaven" and be done for the night. That would be easy, but I would lose a true, teachable moment. I said a quick prayer that I would choose the correct words that she could understand. "God is on His throne in heaven, but because He is God, He is with us all the time too. He is right here in this room with you, now and every night when you sleep. He is in Mommy and Daddy's room too because He can do both at the same time. He goes to the store with us and every other place we go. He is anywhere that you want Him to be." She looked at me with what seemed to be complete understanding. The answer covered her question and she seemed content with it. She put her head back on her pillow and said, "Mommy, can Jesus take a bath with me tomorrow night." I held back a grin because this was clearly a serious question. "Kate, Jesus would love to take a bath with you tomorrow night. Let's remember to invite him", I replied.

It may be funny to think about an invitation for God. I know He doesn't need an invitation, but I hadn't stopped to think if He wants one. God, above all, wants us to choose Him. That is what relationship is all about. If we want more time with God, He is happy to oblige. He knows He is worthy of all praise; He is the only God. He is the only Savior, my strength, my comfort, and my joy. Even though He knows it, I still praise Him for it. If *I* don't praise Him, the rocks will cry out. So, even though He is always with me, shouldn't I invite Him? For that matter, I should ask him to go to school with me, on my way to teach, and to the grocery store where I just might meet someone who needs Him. How much different might the conversation become at my next dinner party if I take the time to invite Him before the other guests. If I spent time on my knees asking God to come into my home as an honored guest, how differently might the evening go?

The reason we as Christians are different is that we have God with us. The gift of the Holy Spirit was left for us so that we might always have God with us. In John, Jesus said that the world cannot receive the Holy Spirit because it neither sees Him nor knows Him (John 14:17). But we know Him because He dwells with us. He is ever present, but He doesn't force us. I have heard people ask, would you be doing that if Jesus were right here with us? I always thought it peculiar because *He is* right here with us. We need to really comprehend that. If there is somewhere in your life that you aren't willing for God to dwell in, then it is time to get rid of that part of your life. Bottom line, no excuses, there should be no place in your life that you feel uncomfortable inviting Jesus.

Now that we have talked about the times we try to avoid Jesus. I need to say that there is no aspect of life that we shouldn't purposefully include Jesus. I don't mean just acknowledging His presence either; I mean purposefully asking for it. John Piper wrote about a vacation they took once where he and his wife practiced this. Here is what he says, "We know he is *always* present with us, as he promised (Matthew 28:20). But it is fitting that we fix our attention on his presence from time to time in a special way, and more consciously include him in the fellowship."

Consciously include Him. Ask Him to join you in even the most mundane activities. Inviting Him can make them anything but mundane. Choosing to invite Him makes them sacred. So the next time you put on a pot of tea and curl up with a good book, ask God to join you...especially if it's His book.

"Where shall I go from your Spirit? Or where shall I flee from your presence? If I ascend to Heaven, you are there! If I make my bed in Sheol, you are there! If I take the wings of the morning and dwell in the other most parts of the sea, even there your hand shall lead me, and your right hand shall hold me."

Psalm 139:7-10

God help me to realize that you want a relationship with me. You are a God who gave his most precious possession, Jesus, just to have a relationship with me. More than anything you want me to choose you. Thank you that you first chose me when I was incapable of giving you anything in return. Thank you for wanting me, just as I am, broken and a mess. You long to be invited in to do your work in me. I invite you into my life and my home and my every thought. Thank you that you will never turn down that kind of invitation.

Notes

Day 7: Repeatedly Ruffled
C.S. Lewis, *The Weight of Glory and other essays,* copyright 1949, C.S. Lewis Pte.Ltd.Copyright renewed 1976, revised 1980 C.S. Lewis Pte.Ltd.

Day 8: I Wanna Hold Your Hand
C. S. Lewis, God in the Dock: *Essays on Theology and Ethics,* 52.

Day 16: The Stench of Leftover Sin
Beth Moore, *A Woman's Heart God's Dwelling Place,* Lifeway Christian Resources copyright 2007, week 4.

Day 27: Whistle While You Work
Elisabeth Elliot, *Through Gates of Splendor,* (Carol Stream, Ill.: Tyndale House, 1986), 20.

Day 30: Fear
C.S. Lewis, *The Screwtape Letters,* Macmillan Company, copyright 1961.

Made in United States
North Haven, CT
08 August 2023

40101420R00071